Hermann Schmidt

The Silver Question in it's Social Aspect

Hermann Schmidt

The Silver Question in it's Social Aspect

ISBN/EAN: 9783744662437

Printed in Europe, USA, Canada, Australia, Japan

Cover: Foto ©Suzi / pixelio.de

More available books at **www.hansebooks.com**

THE SILVER QUESTION
IN ITS SOCIAL ASPECT.

An Enquiry into the Existing Depression of Trade, and the Present Position of the Bi-metallic Controversy.

BY

HERMANN SCHMIDT.

EFFINGHAM WILSON, ROYAL EXCHANGE.

1886.

"Ja! wenn zu Sol sich Luna fein gesellt,
Zum Silber Gold, dann ist es heitere Welt."

GOETHE—*Faust.*

CHANGES and alterations of the most puzzling character have taken place during the last few years in the commerce of the world. To all appearances the causes which produced these changes are still at work. We are witnessing a revolution in prices; a decrease in the opportunities of profit; a decline in the average rate of discount; a rise in all securities of the better class, which bear a fixed interest; a disinclination on the part of capital to embark in productive enterprise; a ·consequent reduction in the chances of employment—entailing misery and suffering on numbers of once prosperous and wealth-producing citizens. Men of science are closely watching these perplexing phenomena; statesmen are anxiously following a development which, to the State, means loss of revenue and reduced resources; a Royal Commission has been enquiring into the origin of a depression unusually wide and unusually prolonged.

The living generation is not unfamiliar with times of difficulties and with crises. But the economic position of to-day is, in many and important respects, undoubtedly different from the cyclical periods of collapse with which the last forty years have made business men acquainted. Those periods were always of limited duration, but there seems to be no end to the present languor ; those depressions extended, generally, only to one or two countries,—where speculation had been carried to excess,—the present covers Europe, America, India, China, Australia, and has not been preceded by any extensive speculation ; formerly, a good harvest went far to remedy the distress ; now, good harvests seem to aggravate the evil. All the hackneyed explanations of political economy, the theories of action and reaction, of ebbing and flowing, of flux and reflux, fail to apply to-day.

But, though to the living generation the spectacle presented by the contemporary economic condition of the world is novel, it would be a mistake to represent the situation as unprecedented. On the contrary, if we turn to history, we find periods extending over many years bearing a close resemblance to our own times, periods in which business was unprofitable, commerce dwindling, and prices falling ; periods in which the wheels of civilization were either at rest, or moving backwards. These were the periods of contracted currencies. Thoughtful students and writers of history have maintained that there is a distinct connection between the rise and fall of enterprise and civilization and the rise and fall of the circulation of the precious metals.[1] The question to be determined is—How far the present distemper of trade is attributable to currency disturbances, and whether it is within our power to find and apply a remedy which will bring stability to prices, breathe new life into torpid commerce, and convert stagnation into activity.

The first fact to be noted is that simultaneously with

[1] " The two greatest events that have occurred in the history of mankind have been directly brought about by a successive *contraction* and *expansion* of the circulating medium of society. The fall of the Roman Empire, so long ascribed in ignorance to slavery, heathenism, and moral corruption, was, in reality, brought about by a decrease in the gold and silver mines of Spain and Greece. Columbus led the way in the career of renovation ; when he spread his sails across the Atlantic he bore mankind and its fortunes in his barque. The annual supply of the precious metals for the use of the globe was tripled. The weight of debt and taxes insensibly wore off under the influence of that prodigious increase."—*Alison.*

" Your Commission asks if similar circumstances ever occurred before. Yes; they occurred after a similar failure of the Roman mines, an event which precipitated the disruption of the Western Empire and was followed by the tremendous consequences so ably depicted in Sir Archibald Alison's *Essays;* they occurred after the dismemberment of Charlemagne's empire, an event which occasioned the secret hoarding of the vast quantities of gold and silver which that monarch had captured in Saxony and Hungary, and had made into money; and they occurred again during the eighteenth century, when the plunder of America and the Orient was quite over, and the metallic product of Spanish America, although it continually increased under the cruel stimulus of the lash, yet failed to increase fast enough to supply a rapidly-growing Europe with the materials for money. In the latter instance the evil effects of diminishing moneys manifested themselves in every country of the world."—*Letter of Alexander Del Mar to Earl of Iddesleigh,* 25th May, 1886.

the commencement of the decline in prices great changes were made in the currencies of some of the leading states of the world.

In 1872 Germany demonetized silver,[1] and adopted the gold standard, and soon later legislation hostile to silver was passed in the United States of America, the States of the Latin Union, Holland, Sweden, Norway, Denmark, and other countries. What we contend is, that there is a connection between this legislation and the present depression of trade. But this contention has to be proved and, in order to do so, we shall have to devote a great part of our work to an exposition of the evil and injurious effects of the demonetization of silver.

From the beginning of this century to the year 1872 the world, as a whole, was bi-metallic. Some countries had adopted the single gold standard, others the single silver standard, a third class—the States comprising the Latin Monetary Union—the double standard, on the basis of $1:15\frac{1}{2}$. A ready means was thus provided for exchanging one metal for the other, and a fixed and stable relation was established between the two metals.[2]

---

[1] When the single gold standard was adopted by Germany it was recommended by nearly all authorities on money and finance who attributed the mercantile superiority of England to her standard and thought that to adopt this standard was a sure way to commercial greatness.

[2] So long as the French Mints were open to the free coinage of both gold and silver the exchange between London and· Calcutta

When, subsequent to 1872, Germany brought her silver to market the Latin Union at first limited, and then suspended, the coinage of that metal. By this means the link that connected gold and silver was snapped. Thenceforward the ratio between these two metals fluctuated according to the accidents of the market. As silver had lost the markets formerly provided for it by the ever open mints of Continental Europe, and as Germany and other countries came in as buyers of gold, the result was a fall in the price of silver.

When this phenomenon first occurred it attracted considerable attention and, in 1876, a Royal Commission examined into it in England. . Its advice was to do nothing, and to allow things to settle themselves. Years have rolled on, and what at first was a comparatively localized difficulty, affecting only the silver market and its immediate connections, has since developed into a disturbance of world-wide extent, affecting the relations between man and man, wherever they are beyond those of mere savages; felt alike by the farmers of England, by the peasants of Russia, by

was virtually as fixed as if it had been based upon one standard only. The fluctuations of this exchange were limited by the two "specie or bullion points," as are at present the fluctuations of the exchange, say, between London and Melbourne. Mr. R. Giffen misinterpreted these oscillations of the silver exchanges between the specie points and the consequent variations of the price of bar silver by citing them as a proof that the French ratio was not always effective.

the wheat growers in Manitoba, by the cotton planters
in South Carolina, and by the squatters in Australia;
disorganizing the Budgets from the Ganges[1] to the
Nile.[2] The words written by William Jacob in 1830,
on the universal fall in prices then happening, seem
indeed again applicable to-day :

"There must be some general cause producing such
extensive effects, which are thus felt alike where tax-
ation is high or low; under despotic and free government;
and whether the land is cultivated by slaves, by serfs,
by hired labourers, or by proprietors."

For a long time it was strenuously denied that this
"general cause, producing such extensive effects,"
could be the demonetization of silver. The connection
between this demonetization and the general fall in
prices was not admitted, and all kind of alternative
theories were put forward to account for the latter.

The extension of postal and telegraphic communica-
tion; the cheapening of freight by land and sea; the
shortening of the distances to be traversed, consequent
on the construction of new railways and canals;
the substitution of steam for sailing power; the exter-
mination of middle men and intermediate agencies;
these and other explanations were given for the lower
prices. There can be no doubt that these forces have

[1] Sir A. Colvin's Indian Financial Statement for 1886-87.

[2] Mr. Edgar Vincent's Report on the Finances of Egypt, 1885-86.

worked to somewhat cheapen commodities—though it is overlooked that if general they ought, in justice, to have tended to similarly cheapen also the production and cost price of gold and silver. A certain fall in prices may, however, we grant, be ascribable to the above influences. But the continuance and the extent of the decline in prices have been so marked and so general, that the insufficiency of the above causes to produce such results is now being gradually admitted, and the connection between the currency question and the increased purchasing power of gold is doubted less and less. Nor do we think that this connection is difficult of demonstration, as the following exposition will prove. This exposition will—in our opinion—have the additional advantage of demonstrating that there are, practically, no assignable limits to the present decline in prices, and that the popular belief that in certain instances the lowest possible level has already been reached is, like so much else, a popular delusion.

The commercial relations affected by a fall in the value of silver are those between the Eastern and the Western world. That trade which, from time immemorial, has been the " world-trade," the possession of which was usually synonymous with empire, is the very one that has been upset by the changed relation of gold to silver. The speculative element introduced into this trade, by the ever varying exchanges, has so often been dwelt upon that we will not enlarge upon it here ; nor do we intend to lay too much stress on the fact that lower exchanges act for a time like a protective barrier against the imports into silver countries, and like a bounty paid on the exports from these countries. The point which, in this connection, is of most importance and which must be specially emphasized, is the influence of the silver countries on the general level of prices in the gold countries.

The relations which here come to the front are those between England and India. India has been developed and protected by English capital for many years past, and for these services she owes a yearly payment to England which, to a very large extent, has to be made on the gold basis. As silver has fallen, the burden of these payments has increased, and India has had to augment her exports to re-establish the balance. The larger offers of her produce resulting from this cause, together with the possibility of obtaining it for less gold, owing to the lower price of silver, brought about the first fall in the prices of the gold countries, which took place in the quotations of the produce of the East. As exchange continued to fall India had to still further increase her exports and, taught by necessity, she began more and more to turn her attention to the cultivation and production of articles which, hitherto, had been chiefly supplied by gold countries, her exports of which would therefore enjoy to the full the benefit of the lower price of silver, *i.e.*, wheat, cotton, hides, etc.

The larger exports of raw cotton affected principally the interests of the United States of America, but the larger exports of wheat produced important results in Europe—for they mark the origin and beginning of the general decline of the prices of agricultural produce in the West. In vain have continental states endeavoured to neutralize this fall by re-enacting corn laws ; the fall in the price of silver has, hitherto, invariably outrun the agricultural imposts. European farmers, finding wheat unprofitable, began to grow other produce with the result of extending further the fall of prices: the greater cultivation of beet-root in Austria and Germany, for instance, producing the collapse in the sugar market; the greater attention of farmers to dairy produce bringing down its prices.

We have, thus far, only considered the influence of the silver-using East as a producer and exporter on the prices in the gold countries. Its influence, however, as a consumer and importer is not less potent. The purchasing power of silver, in the East, not having materially altered, all the articles which are manu-factured in gold countries for export to the silver countries had to decline in price with the fall of the rupee and the dollar. We are, for instance, inclined to attribute the fall in raw cotton more to the fact that cotton goods are so largely consumed in the East that their price is, to a great extent, dictated by the silver countries than to the other fact that India's raw cotton

can now compete at lower gold prices with that of the
United States and Egypt owing to the lower exchange.

Being in this manner attacked from two sides, the
stability of prices in the gold countries has given way
all round. "The fall extended to, and successively embraced, wider and wider areas according to the law of
precession of prices."[1] This is not the place to follow
this precession in detail, but we may remark that, in
consequence of the great fall of agricultural produce,
both rent and land have receded in price and that,
following the ramification of this precession still
further, the general fall in prices rendered it impossible
for some countries—recently, for instance, Roumania
and the Argentine Republic—to keep their currency at
par with gold, thus plunging these countries into the
abyss of inconvertible paper money, and lowering, in its
turn, for a time the gold value of their exports. As an
example, we may mention the case of wool, which was
one of the articles that resisted longest the fall in
prices, but which was brought down when the River
Plate countries suspended specie payments.[2] This

---

[1] Because this precession has not always been as regular as
clockwork, M. P. Leroy Beaulieu denies the connection between the
fall in prices and the silver question. *(Revue des deux mondes,
Mai,* 1886.) With the same arguments the influence of increased
issues of inconvertible paper on prices has always been denied by
inflationists.

[2] More recently there has been some recovery from the lowest
prices reached, simultaneously with a decline of the premium on
gold at Buenos Ayres.

event again reacted most unfavourably on the prosperity of gold mono-metallic Australia.

We thus find, all the world over, a close and demonstrable connection between the demonetization of silver and the fall in gold prices. *But the fall in gold prices is the appreciation of gold.* This appreciation is, therefore, primarily not so much a cause as an effect,[1] it is the result of the fall in silver, and simply the phenomenon of a general fall in prices which the fall in silver brings about, stated inversely.

This exposition establishes the fact which we wish specially to emphasize, that a rise in the purchasing power of gold can take place without any reference to the abundance or the scarcity of that metal. Very able writers, such as Professors de Laveleye and J. S. Nicholson, as well as Mr. Moreton Frewen, have laid great stress on what is known as the " Quantitäts-Theorie," and on the present scarcity of gold. With them we think that the arguments based on gold scarcity have great weight, and we, also, think that those gentlemen have largely succeeded in proving a real scarcity. For, consequent on the demonetization of silver, a much larger demand has arisen for gold which, coupled with a decreasing production, is now accelerating the downward movement of silver and,

---

[1] Mr. Harvey expressed the same opinion : "I agree that the appreciation of gold is more an effect than a cause of low prices."—*Journal of Institute of Bankers*, June, 1886.

consequently, of prices in general. The " Quantitäts-Theorie," therefore, enters after all into this question, not in a direct, but in an indirect manner.[1] And it is certain to do so much more, should the course of events force one or more other nations to melt down part of their over-valued legal tender silver coins, still in circulation, and sell them for gold. It is then that the question of gold scarcity will, indeed, become the all-important factor in this controversy. We think, however, it is better and facilitates a thorough understanding of the question before us, if we always bear in mind that the depreciation of silver will account for the appreciation of gold without reference to the circulating quantity of the latter metal.[2] This circumstance is very instructive. It will teach us that those leaders of opinion are far from grasping the subject who think that they have demolished the bi-metallic argument because it assumes " that the principal cause of the fall in values since 1873 is scarcity of gold,"[3] and because they fancy they are able to show that this gold scarcity does not exist. It will teach us that we should

[1] Dr. Otto Arendt, in his *Währungsstreit* comes to the same conclusion, though he uses the term "indirect" in a slightly different sense from that in which it is used here.

[2] The following remarks of Mr. Cernuschi express this idea in its extreme : " If by an enchanter's wand all the silver francs, all the silver marks, all the silver dollars, were converted into gold francs, gold marks, gold dollars, the European and American prices would remain unchanged."—Letter to *Economist*, 24th April, 1886.

[3] See letter of Mr. W. Fowler to *Times*, 18th of August, 1886.

be trusting to uncertain guides indeed if we attempted to apply to a world-wide calamity such local remedies as the issue of £1 notes.[1] It will teach us that the real remedy, whatever it be, must be a cure, not only for the scarcity of gold, but, above all, for the depreciation of silver; must in fact re-establish the dislocated par between gold and silver.

This explanation will, we are convinced, sufficiently prove the fact that the general level of gold prices depends upon the price of silver. As already admitted, other causes may be responsible for part of the fall in prices that has taken place, but the depreciation of silver remains the general and the chief cause.[2] From this it follows that as long as silver has not arrived at its lowest possible price, as long as there is room or margin for a further fall of that metal, there cannot be any finality in the general fall of prices. "With each fresh tumble of silver a lower deep must be reached."[3]

This is a conclusion of the gravest importance for practical business men which will satisfactorily explain some otherwise unaccountable events. During the

[1] Proposed by Mr. Ch. Gairdner.—*Journal of Institute of Bankers,* March, 1886.

[2] Mr. D. Barbour in his able *Theory of Bi-metallism* arrives at the conclusion that if the appreciation of gold, plus depreciation of silver, amounts to 19 %, the more probable supposition is that gold prices have been kept down by $9\frac{1}{4}$ % and silver prices kept higher by $9\frac{1}{2}$ %. If our demonstration is correct nearly the whole of that 19 % would be appreciation of gold.

[3] *New York Chronicle,* 29th May, 1886.

last ten years it has often been asserted that a certain article had "touched bottom," since it sold already below cost price. By-and-bye this article was sold at a fresh reduction of 5 or 10 per cent. What had happened? Silver had experienced a further decline, some raw material could be imported from the East at lower prices owing to lower exchanges, and the former calculations no longer applied. There was therefore room for the market to go down, and it did so. The apostles of the classic political economy, the devotees of cheapness, were afforded an opportunity of pointing to another instance of reduced cost of production, to a fresh triumph of civilization over the forces of nature !

This exposition shows the utter fallacy of expecting a sound and lasting improvement in trade before the fall in silver is arrested. Till this is finally done the trade of the world in general, and of England in particular, must and will decline. Even the opening up of new markets, so often preached as a panacea, would, as Professor Nicholson has pointed out,[1] give no relief, unless, which is not likely, they bring new supplies of gold, for extension of commerce would mean increased demand on bullion and a further fall in prices.

This is, no doubt, a very unpalatable and disagreeable truth to those self-proclaimed economists who, not distinguishing between low prices and low cost of production, between a fall in money prices, and a fall in

[1] *The Silver Question*, 1886.   .

real prices, praise the present as a time of "cheapness and of plenty." Alas! their so called cheapness is nothing but dearness of gold, and their plenty, where it is real, testifies only to the reduced capacity of the masses at large to command and consume the commodities which, when produced, were intended for the benefit of the whole human race.

Having thus traced the connection between the demonetization of silver and the fall in prices we now approach the question, whether such a fall in prices is really an evil. Some have denied and others doubted this. The argument of those who can see no harm in the appreciation of gold is as follows :

" If two sovereigns at the present value of gold have the same purchasing power which three sovereigns used to have, the obvious result is that two sovereigns will serve just as well as three used to serve. Thus by natural causes there comes an economy of gold to the precise extent to which there exists a need for it. The balance is self-adjusting." [1]

If money were nothing but a counter for effecting exchanges this view would be correct, but as it is the standard in which all monetary obligations are contracted, such reasoning is inadmissible. It is this standard function of money which we have ever to keep in

[1] *Times,* 12th March, 1886.

B

view when considering the demonetization of silver and the evils which it has wrought.

Indeed it is here that we touch the most important point in the whole currency controversy, the very kernel of this " Silver Question." Our opponents know this very well, for " if money possessed really no other qualifications than that of a railroad, or a steam ship, or a bill of exchange, if it simply exchanged one commodity for another, the creditor class in this or other countries would never make Rome howl with its denunciations of silver." Nor does the importance of this standard function of money decrease with the progress of civilization. On the contrary, the greater the development of a country the more important will be this function, the more numerous the monetary relations of the citizens. It is through this close connection between silver and the stability of the gold standard that the silver question becomes of such paramount interest to all gold countries, where, indeed, it is one of the greatest and most influential of social factors.[1]

Viewed thus as a question affecting the living organism of society the appreciation of gold means an altera-

---

[1] The champions of the old mercantile theory who endeavoured to prevent the export and encouraged the import of the precious metals, have often been laughed at since the days of Adam Smith. However, if their object was to keep the supply of money constant and prevent a disturbance in the standard they were, perhaps, wiser than some of their critics.

tion in the standard of value. The first, the foremost requisite of every standard—stability—disappears.[1] A standard that has confessedly altered 25 to 30 $^0/_0$ in the course of a decade is really a standard no longer. Though not possessed of an ounce of full legal tender silver, England finds thus her standard engulfed in the silver difficulty. This is why the price of silver is of such enormous importance to England. And our readers will now be able to appraise at their true value the ability, the knowledge, the perception, and the scientific competence of those leaders of public opinion who boldly declare that England, having a gold standard, need not care what becomes of silver.

The evils resulting from an appreciating standard are ubiquitous and too numerous to be depicted in detail, but we will glance at the most prominent of them, sufficiently to bear out our contention, that to all gold countries the silver question is at bottom a social question.[2]

[1] All who admit that there is not enough gold in the world to entirely do away with silver desire the standard to remain stable. For, if stability were of no consequence, any quantity of gold would do, all that is required would be a corresponding fall in prices. In that sense it is perfectly true that money, like water, will always find its own level.

[2] Not only in England but on the Continent the opponents of bi-metallism overlook this point. They think they are safe from the effects of the silver difficulty if they accumulate sufficient gold. This error explains why in Germany the gold mono-metallists speak of the " relatively very satisfactory position of Germany in the currency question."

The effect of an appreciating standard upon trade is immediate.

Merchants who find that in consequence of a gradual decline of prices their ventures result in losses will prefer restricting business or retiring from it altogether to continuing such trading. Manufacturers who are unable to obtain for the finished article a price that will leave a margin of profit, or even repay cost of production, will after a period of unequal struggle close their mills. Small traders who find stock continually declining in value will keep as little of it on hand as possible. Everywhere the money losses will disseminate a feeling of disappointment and discouragement which it would be useless to attempt to combat with the philosophic reflection that though as expressed in money the capital has diminished, it remains, in truth, as large as ever or nearly so because the purchasing power of money has increased.

That a good deal of the depression of trade is ascribable to these causes cannot be doubted. Nor can it be questioned that if of late socialistic difficulties have come again more to the front the reason must be looked for in the diminished opportunity of the employment of labour consequent on the decline of general activity. And if it has also become less easy for statesmen to maintain friendly relations between the different nations the same facts must partly be held responsible, for the history of the world proves nothing more than that race hostilities grow with commercial or industrial depression.

The effect of an appreciating standard on contracts is scarcely less immediate than that on trade, and certainly not less important ; for " in a highly civilized modern society all the production and all the distribution of wealth depend on a complicated and vast series of contracts which are all expressed in terms of money." The tendency of the alteration which those contracts undergo through the appreciation of gold will be to benefit the economically strong at the expense of the economically weak; the economically idle at the expense of the economically busy ; in short to favor the creditor at the expense of the debtor. No doubt the lower rate of interest which in times of depressed state of trade generally prevails will allow some of the debtors to rectify to a partial extent this injustice, but the injustice itself will remain. But if the weight of debt becomes heavier it is equivalent to a real increase in the fixed charges. Thus under an appreciating standard not only individuals but also governments suffer, the latter through the decrease in the yield of such imposts as income tax and probate and legacy duties as well as through the influence of a general depression on customs and excise. Government expenditure is, on the other hand, difficult to curtail, a reduction of official salaries which justice demands is not easily affected, and only few countries are in a position to lower their debt charges by "conversions."[1] Throughout all these changes, people with fixed incomes enjoy unjust benefits. If the charge of "unearned increment" is to find a place in political economy it is here that it should be preferred, it is against the capitalists, the owners of the mobilized wealth, that it should be levelled.

There would be a redeeming feature in these social changes if thereby the working men had also obtained any economic advantages. Unfortunately, however, they have not. To suppose, like Mr. Hansard,[2] that this has been the case implies a misconception of the whole phenomenon.[3] Depressed trade reduces the opportu-

[1] As an instance that in spite of reducing the amount of debt and lowering the rate of interest payable on the remainder, the debt charge measured by its demand on labor may increase, we may cite the case of United States of America. According to Mr. Moreton Frewen the United States have from 1865 to 1886 reduced their debt from over £500,000,000 to less than £300,000,000. But while in 1865 18 million bales of cotton or 25 million tons of bar iron would have wiped out the total debt, it would take to-day 32 million bales of cotton or 35 million tons of bar iron to pay off what remains, i.e., little more than half of the original amount. The *effective increase* which must have taken place during the last 15 years in the debt charge of states which like Russia, Austria, France, Hungary, Australia have largely augmented the total debt, must seriously interfere with the prosperity of these countries.

[2] It will be a distinct advantage if the present appreciation caused by the low level of prices continues *and wages or incomes remain the same.*—"Essay on prices of some commodities during the decade 1874 to 1883," *Journal of Institute of Bankers*, January, 1885.

[3] In America, and elsewhere, the gold advocates have adopted the tactics of pleading against silver in the interest of the working man. This touching taking-to-heart of the welfare of the labourers by those who, as a class, have ever been oblivious of their interests

nities of employment with the inevitable result, sooner or later of lowering wages.[1] The action of Trades Unions may for a time obscure this issue, but it cannot prevent it, for even where they are able to keep up the nominal scale of remuneration of labor, they cannot guarantee continuous employment on these terms. Mr. Giffen has shown a clearer perception of this part of the question than Mr. Hansard; he perceived the inevitable drift of events and concluded his essay, "Further Notes on the Progress of the Working Classes,"[2] with a warning to them, "that they should be prepared to some extent for a reduction in money wages."

The greatest, and let me add, perhaps, the most innocent sufferers, however, through an appreciating standard are the landed interests. With the competition of silver using countries in the wheat markets,[3]

has, however, not had the desired effect. Senator Teller said in United States Congress; "This pretence of interest in the wages of the labouring man is not only weak, deceiving no one, but it is false."—*Speech*, 19th January, 1886.

[1] There is little doubt that this is already happening. On 17th April, 1886 the *Economist* sums up the situation as follows : "The yield of the income tax is diminishing, the working classes are less fully employed than before, and are earning less when employed, and pauperism, notwithstanding all that trade societies are doing to support their idle members, is increasing.

[2] *Journal of Statistical Society*, March, 1886.

[3] The question whether Indian wheat exports will be stopped if exchange should rise again is frequently put, but difficult to answer. It is quite possible that to a large extent this export might continue, although in its infancy it was greatly assisted if not called into being by the fall in exchange. But, and that is the great point

and the consequent fall in prices of agricultural produce all round, farmers cannot make both ends meet, and the result is a fall in rents and in the value of land.[1] After the ruin of the farmers, if the current of events be not reversed, will come that of the landlords. Translated into their language the triumph of gold mono-metallism means " No Rent."

Of course it would be contrary to the spirit of the age, at least in England, to say a word in defence not only of landlords but of landlordism. Little indeed is thought of the injustice of any social development if land be the suffering party. But we may here remark. that as popular a writer as J. S. Mill looks upon a rise in rents as indicative of the progressive state of society,[2] and that so impartial an authority as J. Locke considered falling rents a sign of decay.[3] And it is the banishment of silver that is producing the present fall of rents in England.

which interests agriculturists, even should wheat continue to come after exchange has risen, it could do so only at higher gold prices.

[1] Sir James Caird reckons the total loss last year (1885) to the landed interest in England in spendable income at more than £40,000,000. (Committee on Depression of Trade.) The net assessment of landed property for 1884-85 show a decline of £5,000,000 against those of 1879-80. Capitalizing this at thirty years' purchase, we have a total depreciation in the capital value of land of £150,000,000.—*Economist*, 21st November, 1885.

[2] *Principles of Political Economy*, iv., 3.

[3] "An infallible sign of your decay of wealth is the falling of rents, and the raising of them would be worth the nation's care."— *Value of Money.*

On the continent where landed interests do not enjoy such unpopularity as in this country, the government having observed the destruction with which "land" is menaced, decided to come to its aid. Being still too deeply committed to the "battle of the standards" and as yet, therefore, unable to apply the remedy—the rehabilitation of silver—they have reintroduced the duties on agricultural produce, a proceeding which is perfectly logical and which for a time at least brings, if not cure, at all events relief.[1]

The gold standard has thus become the principal and the most powerful cause of that revival of protectionism[2] which has so much surprised a world which thought that the years of Cobden Club propaganda would have shown better results. But continental statesmen know very well why they have come to the rescue of their agriculture. For not only does agriculture still represent the largest industry of their different countries, it is also considered to be of great political importance as furnishing a constant supply of healthy and strong

[1] In England, agricultural depression is often looked upon as a visitation of Providence, against which human wisdom availeth not. Thus, in a leading article of 11th of January, 1886, the *Standard* says : "Country gentlemen who are suffering from no fault of their own, but from one of those dispensations of nature which no wisdom can avoid."

[2] Mr. Giffin, when looking around for the most effective weapon against bi-metallism, boldly declared it to be "Protection."—(*On some Bi-metallic Fallacies.*) Our readers are able to appreciate the appropriateness of such an expression. Even the *Economist* could not swallow that pill.

specimens of humanity, and of developing among large classes of society that feeling of true conservatism which forms an invaluable counterpoise to the restless population of the great towns, so often *rerum novarum cupidi.*

But the social influences of an appreciating standard embrace even wider areas than those considered so far. According to Mr. Parnell[1] the whole Irish Question is at bottom a question of the value of agricultural produce. According to Herr von Kardorff[2] the anti-semitic movement in Germany is to a large extent the expression of the antagonism of the Teuton landlord to the Jewish mortgagee, whose mortgage is seen to be constantly increasing in value and increasing to the detriment and at the expense of the mortgagor. Similar considerations account for the strong partisanship of the capitalist classes, the owners of the mobilized wealth, in Europe and still more in America —where this question is better understood—for the gold standard. They explain the favour with which this standard is on the whole regarded by the bourses and the stock exchanges, the markets for this mobilized wealth.

But not only the capitalist classes are in favor of the gold standard, the revolutionary leaders[3] are so too,

[1] Speech in House of Commons, February, 1886.

[2] Speech in Reichstag, 6th March, 1885.

[3] The most intelligent and far-seeing leader of Social Democracy

though for different reasons. As the latter live on discontent, they naturally oppose everything which, like the rehabilitation of silver, will improve the social condition of the masses and increase the general contentment.

To sum up: the evils produced in gold countries by the demonetization of silver are social; a violent and gratuitous subversion of the historic relation of class to class,[1] a silent but powerful revolution, a wholesale confiscation of the property of the industrious for the benefit of the non-industrious, a sure ultimate deterioration of the position of the working classes, a re-opening of the disputes between debtors and creditors which all through history have been the chief topics of demagogic and socialistic agitation.

How the different classes of society are affected by these changes we need not here discuss. What we have stated suffices, we think, to establish the immense social and political importance of this Silver Question. But it is perhaps worthy of remark that among the sufferers from this disturbance are the custodians of capital—the bankers.[2] A low rate of interest consequent on declining

in Germany, Herr Bebel, spoke last year, in the diet of Saxony, against bi-metallism.

[1] "Money is related to equity or to the maintenance of equitable relations between capital and labour."—A. Del Mar, *Money in civilization.*

[2] No doubt there are other classes than the bondholders who benefit by the greater purchasing power of gold. The *Economist*

trade is a feature of the situation, for holders of money are anxious to *lend*, but not to *buy*. Through this cause even the capitalists will eventually be losers and sufferers.[1] The far-seeing capitalist, therefore, who knows that ultimately his prosperity depends upon the general prosperity of the country, has no reason to champion an appreciating standard,[2] no reason to uphold an economic condition which, instead of presenting the characteristics of prosperous times, high wages, and high interest, shows the very opposite features : low interest and low wages.[3]

It may probably be thought that if the fall in silver is such a misfortune to the gold countries it must by contrast be an advantage to the silver using countries. There are not wanting advocates who maintain this view, and it must be admitted that, owing to the fall in exchange, the silver countries have nearly entirely escaped the principal evil from which the gold countries are suffering

(10th of April, 1886,) mentions as such the brewers. According to the Chairman of the National Discount Co., (speech, 20th January, 1886,) " The low rate of money, which had been so adverse to the banking interests, is not unprofitable to bill brokers."

[1] Alison maintains that the contraction of currency which attended the resumption of specie payments by Bank of England, in 1821 caused as much loss to money capitalists by lowering the rate of interest as to producers by lowering the price of commodities.

[2] The traditional policy of the Rothschilds has been in favour of the double standard.

[3] " A low rate of interest is a symptom of a great accumulation of capital; but it is, also, a sympton of a low rate of profits and of an *advancement to a stationary state*."—*D. Ricardo, On Protection to Agriculture.*

—that of an appreciating standard. Silver prices have remained fairly steady. It must be further admitted that, under the stimulating influence of cheap silver, the export and import trade of the silver using countries has developed or at least been spared that retrogression which exists in the gold countries.

Let us take the case of India. Though the prices of Indian produce in Europe have fallen, India continues to receive for them nearly the same number of rupees as before. Owing to the fall in exchange she has thus been spared that fall in prices which is the bane of the gold countries.[1] Moreover under the influence of the low exchange, mills and manufactures are being established in India which compete under advantageous conditions with those of the gold countries and add to the national wealth. For it is clear that an exchange of 1s. 6d. per rupee instead of the former 2s. means *ceteris paribus* not only an import duty 25 % on all goods from gold countries, but also an export bonus of 33 % on all goods sent to gold countries. However, as a matter of fact, neither such a restriction of the imports nor such a stimulus to the exports has for any length of time actually occurred, for the equilibrium has always been quickly re-established by a readjustment of prices, a readjustment which, as we have shown above, took the form

[1] " If then it is asked what effect exchange has had on trade the answer is, that it has saved the trade of India, in the face of the low prices ruling in European markets, from disaster."—*Minute of Mr. J. E. O'Conor*, Simla, 13th July, 1886.

of a fall in the gold prices.[1]   From this it is clear that
if under such circumstances the advantage of the Indian
exporter and the Indian manufacturer over their European or American competitors is to continue, the
exchange will have to *keep continually falling*, a process which by its very nature cannot go on indefinitely.

But though so long as we confine our enquiry into
the effect of the silver depreciation on India to purely
commercial considerations, as we have done so far, it
may appear doubtful whether on balance India gains or
loses by that depreciation, we fear that there will be no
longer a doubt on this question as soon as we extend our
survey a little further.

India has contracted large gold obligations both on
government and private account, the burden of which in-
creases as silver falls.   Whatever profits greater activity
of trade and increased industry may have brought
to India, they are, unquestionably, being more than
absorbed in providing for the loss by the fall of exchange
on the gold remittances.   As it is the Indian government on which a great part of this loss falls, the causes
of these currency disturbances have been minutely in-
vestigated by the Indian officials, and as a consequence
we find that next to the American Statesmen those of
India are to-day best informed on the silver question.

---

[1] It can fearlessly be asserted that few economists have foreseen
such a result.   What was generally expected was a re-establishment
of the equilibrium by a rise in silver prices.

Another drawback of the present situation in India consists in the fact that the fall in exchange severely impedes the influx of British capital into that country.[1] It is known that the Anglo-Indian banks have " brought home " their sterling deposits and that they are at present trying to do the same for their capital. This explains the continuance of high rate of interest in Bombay and Calcutta, whilst money money goes a-begging in Lombard Street.

This circumstance is not without political significance. Should the peace of India ever be endangered by a serious foe and the government of that country be under the necessity of raising a large loan it could do so only in Europe and in gold. That under the present conditions a large increase in the gold liabilities of India would simply be financial ruin is evident after the experience of the course of exchange during the last few years. We touch here undoubtedly the weakest joint in the armour of England's great dependency, an armour which so many sacrifices have been made to perfect.

We have entered more minutely into this question of Indian exchange because the subject is somewhat com-

---

[1] " When the Port Commissioners of Calcutta attempted to raise a loan of 75 lakhs of rupees, in September, 1885, guaranteed by the Government of India, the total amount of tenders was only R40,200, and no portion of this insignificant amount was offered at par."— *Despatch of Government of India,* 2nd February, 1886. This loan carried 5 % interest.

plicated and not always correctly understood. On broad grounds, however, the question, whether the International depreciation of the currency of a country is a benefit to that country or not, need not be. discussed at length, for the answer admits of no doubt. Such a depreciation must be an evil or else the countries with the most depreciated currencies would be economically the most prosperous and financially the soundest in the world, and nothing more propitious could happen to India than the fall of the rupee to the value of 6d. or, still better, to that of the cowrie shell.

But there is for India still greater danger a-head. If in the West the crusade against silver goes on successfully much longer, it is only a question of time when silver will be entirely discarded by Europe and America. India's currency would then no longer have International value and India would be again relegated to the position in which she found herself before 1766 with her copper standard, and from which she was rescued by the wisdom of English administrators. It is the clear duty of Indian Statesmen to prevent such a consummation.[1] To neglect

[1] Rather than allow this to pass the Indian Government would have to close the mints to the free coinage of silver, and coin the necessary money itself. Such a measure, it is true, would not establish any link between the Indian and the Western currencies, but it would allow the Government some control over its standard of value. Austria and Russia have adopted this policy. By its large sales of exchange the Indian Government would have special advantages in controlling its currency. There are objections to such a step, based on the commercial relations of India to China, but in a great emer-

this duty either through carelessness or through an ignorant adherence to English mono-metallic theories would be to perpetrate a cruel wrong on the people of India; a wrong which would assuredly one day be followed by historic retribution.

Not only the gold countries, then, but also the silver countries suffer from the demonetization of silver. To gold countries it has brought the appreciation of the standard, which the Continent endeavours to counteract by protective duties, through which in free-trading England the boundary line of cultivation is receding, and by which in America the whole farming interest of the South and the West is summoned to the banners of the silver party.[1] In silver countries it has embarrassed and threatens to ruin the National Finances. Throughout the world it is unsettling contracts and disturbing the social relations of humanity.

Before leaving this part of our subject it would, we

genoy they would have to be set aside.—The proposal to introduce a gold standard into India could be supported as giving that country an International money, but it would be open to all the objections based on the commercial relations of India with China, and the other silver countries. Moreover, a gold valuation would subject India to all the misfortunes of an appreciating standard, and to all the social evils of a general fall in prices,—a fall which the demand of gold for India would intensify to a fearful degree. If the fear of bi-metallism should drive our opponents to accept this policy as a remedy, they must indeed be *in extremis.*

[1] In the division of the Morrison resolution in the House of Representatives, before its adjournment in August, 1886, out of fifty seven Western Republicans fifty one voted on the silver side, joining the forty one Western Democrats who voted solid.

C

think, be desirable to inquire how far the above state-ments tally with the text books of political economy. As the phenomenon of the silver depreciation had not occurred when most of these books were written, we are not surprised that this subject is not specially com-mented on by them. They treat, however, of the some-what analagous case of depreciated paper currencies. According to them a depreciated currency will not affect the International commerce of a country, because prices in that country would rise in the same proportion as the currency depreciates. This statement leaves the highly important factor of the International indebtedness of such a country entirely out of consideration and must therefore be declared incomplete. As to the case which we have been considering there is no doubt that nothing of the kind described above has happened. Prices in the silver countries have admittedly not risen, and the equilibrium of trade has therefore not been re-established in the manner which the text books lead us to anticipate. But we even doubt whether conditions such as would produce a rise in prices exist in the silver countries. The imports of silver for instance into India between 1871 and 1885, in spite of the lower quotations for that metal in London, were less than those between 1856 and 1870.[1] The coinage of silver in India during the former was also smaller than during the latter years. The totals, it is true, are still large; but in this con-

---

[1] Net imports of silver, 1856-70 £147,350,000; 1871-85, £81,002,000
   Coinage   „   „   £130,120,000 ;   „   £82,411,000

nection the wide extent of India must be borne in mind as well as the prevailing Eastern habits of hoarding the precious metals.

We thus find the text books at fault all around, utterly unable to satisfactorily interpret the existing state of affairs, or to explain how a currency can be internationally depreciated, and yet retain its purchasing power at home unimpared. We think, therefore, we are justified if under these circumstances we do not attach much importance to the fact that these ponderous authorities are at variance with us. But the duty of carefully examining the objections raised against our theory of gold appreciation remains, a duty which we now propose to perform.

The first objection to our theory is not against the fact of gold appreciation but against the importance which we have attributed to it as regards a country such as England. It is admitted by our opponents that other nations, both with a gold and with a silver standard, may suffer through the demonetization of silver, but it is denied that such can be the case with England, because she is a creditor nation and therefore benefits rather than loses by the appreciation of gold. This view was expressed years ago in the columns of the leading city paper and was lately repeated in all seriousness by an ex-cabinet minister.[1] That there is an advantage accruing to a nation by the appreciation of gold from

---

[1] Speech of Mr. Shaw-Lefevre, *Journal Institute of Bankers*, June, 1886.

its foreign gold investments cannot be denied, but it must be of very doubtful value, for the causes which make gold-debts more valuable render also the debtor less able to pay, and if repudiation should ever become popular it would be by the knowledge that the creditor deliberately secures unjust advantages and it would be by arguments such as the above. But our foregoing exposition has already disclosed the utter inadequacy of the above reason for deeming the appreciation of gold an advantage, cynically selfish though this reason be. If, as we contend, the evil consequences of an appreciating standard are loss of trade and social disorganization inflicted on all classes alike, they are of such importance that any gain on the foreign gold investments, pocketed as it is by a single class, counts as nothing in comparison.

The second objection to the theory of gold appreciation calls that appreciation itself into question. The fall in prices is admitted, but the appreciation of the standard is denied, apparently without perceiving the fact that the two are identical. The objection is put in the form of the following question: "How can gold be appreciated when money remains cheap?" Now this objection sounds very plausible, but all the same it rests upon a fallacy, a fallacy so frequent that J. S. Mill actually quotes it as an illustration of the fallacies of confusion.[1] The confusion is that of the two meanings

[1] *System of Logic,* ii., 7.

of " money " : *Currency* and *capital seeking investment.* As to the question whether a low rate of interest must be accompanied by a low purchasing power of money, the same author answers it by saying[1] that " the rate of interest bears no necessary relation to the quantity or value of the money in circulation." Another authority[2] expresses the same idea as follows:—" The fall or rise of interest making neither more nor less land, money or any sort of commodity, alters not at all the value of money in reference to commodities" *i.e.,* its purchasing power. As for the influence of the increased purchasing power of money on interest, if it has any effect at all, it should be towards lower rates. A change from a greater to a less quantity of money makes the money in the hands of lenders more valuable, the tendency of the rate of interest will therefore be towards a fall. This is what is happening now.[3] This tendency is accentuated by the general desire, existing in falling markets, to lend money rather than to invest it productively.[4] It is counteracted from time to time by scares about the insufficiency of the gold reserves in the banks. To

---

[1] *Principles of Political Economy,* iii., 13.

[2] J. Locke, *Value of Money.*

[3] The Directors of the *Deutsche Bank,* in their Report for 1885, very tersely describe the situation: "Owing to the universal decline in prices, less money has been required in connection with the purchase and distribution of raw material and manufactured goods, but the surplus capital arising from this state of affairs has failed to find other commercial employment."

[4] The less gold there is the more it will appear superabundant, for the less there is the less it is required."—*Prof. de Laveleye.*

these preoccupations we owe certain spasms of dear
money, the curious spectacle of high bank rates and but
few bills offered for discount. During the last few
years we have on several occasions witnessed that the
Bank of England put up its rate and then itself created
a demand for money by borrowing in the market on
consols. The machinery destined to check overtrading
was in these instances set in motion, in the absence of
almost any trade demand, in order to protect the gold.

In this connection we may inquire into the value of
the statement which is sometimes made in refutation of
the theory of gold scarcity that the reserves of the great
National banks show on the whole no decline of strength.
As an argument in this controversy this statement carries
no weight. The smaller demand for trade purposes has
caused some of the gold which used to circulate to return
to the vaults of the banks, but this gain of these
institutions represents only loss of the circulation.
Moreover we must not overlook the fact that outside of
England a considerable part of the reserves of State
banks consists of legal tender silver valued at the former
high prices and therefore of but doubtful efficacy in
cases of emergency.

But the most serious objection to the theory of gold
appreciation is that hard money is really no longer the
important factor it used to be in the economics of trade
and in determining prices, because trade is more and
more carried on by substitutes for money,—the bank

note and the cheque. It must be observed that this objection is entirely based upon the "Quantitäts Theorie." The argument is that even admitting an actual scarcity of gold there need be no appreciation of that metal if the credit system had become more perfected, whilst our contention is that even were there no scarcity of gold, its appreciation would follow through the fall in silver. This objection does not therefore touch our case at all and might consequently be dismissed without any more remark. But we will go further in meeting our opponents. We will express the opinion that even if the fall of silver did not influence at present the purchasing power of gold money, the theory of our opponents is untenable. We admit that credit to a certain extent fulfils the functions of money. But we do not admit their further argu-ments. A formula of political economy runs as follows : " Prices vary *ceteris paribus* inversely to the quantity of money multiplied by its rapidity of circulation."[1] If this rapidity could be increased with every decrease in the quantity of money, if every withdrawal of hard cash could be at once replaced by "representative" money, our opponents would be right. But credit is a plant of slow and tender growth. There are real limits to an expansion of credit, limits which vary with the state of trade and the degree of commercial development of a country, but which for the time being, cannot be ex-

---

[1] Consult John Locke, J. S. Mill, and others.

ceeded to any considerable extent. The reduction of cash therefore lessens the actual total money even under the credit system. In fact under this system the actual money is lessened to a greater extent than where no credit exists, because it is reduced not only by the real specie withdrawals, but also by the re-calling of the representative money which was based on that specie.[1] There is no doubt that if silver had remained money, the circulation of the world would have had the benefit, not only of the silver itself, but also of the credit money which would have been built upon that silver.

The returns of the bankers' clearing house in London are a proof that the representative money was not augmented when gold became scarcer.[2] There is no perceptible increase in these figures during the last twelve

[1] A comparison between the effect of gold arrivals or withdrawals on the money markets of London and Paris will illustrate this. In London, where the credit system is highly perfected, £5,000,000 gold more or less in the bank reserve will make a difference of 2 to 4% in the bank rate; in Paris the same amount has sometimes not even produced ½ % change.

[2] In 1869 the *Economist* stated that a yearly production of gold of £30,000,000 was scarcely sufficient to cope with the growing transactions of commerce. Since that time silver has been extensively demonetized, and the gold production has fallen to £16-17,000,000. According to Professors Soetbeer and de Laveleye there is now a surplus of only about £1,000,000 in the yearly gold budget of the world, after allowing for consumption in arts and absorption by the East. This £1,000,000 has to perform the duty which seventeen years ago, according to the *Economist*, required £30,000,000 for a smaller area.

years.[1] Business men have evidently been too prudent to extend the superstructure of credit while the base was shrinking and though there can be little doubt that during this period commercial transactions have increased, the adjustment had to be brought about by a reduction in prices. Everywhere the same spectacle!

But our opponents have not contented themselves with objections to our theory. They have put forth an explanation of their own of the present economic condition. We will now proceed to an examination of this alternative theory, persuaded that if we could prove its insufficiency and hollowness, we shall enlist converts to our own creed.

The facts which according to the mono-metallists account entirely for the lower prices, have already been alluded to. Better communications, quicker transit by land and water, saving of the use of capital by means of telegrams and otherwise, diminution of stocks. In fact the fall in prices is represented to be a fall "due to the ingenuity and energy of man."[2] Nobody will deny that those influences tend to lower real prices. But as they are universal they ought, as we said, to tend to lower the prices of the precious metals, *i.e.*, of money, and

---

[1] Total amount cleared :

1874	£5,937,000,000	1883	£5,929,000,000
1875	£5,686,000,000	1884	£5,799,000,000
1876	£4,963,000,000	1885	£5,518,000,000

[2] Mr. W. Fowler's speech, *Journal Institute of Bankers*, June, 1886 ; and also his letter to *Times*, 16th August, 1886.

thereby in a rough manner, re-establish the equilibrium by restoring the old level of prices. This they have admittedly not done. Moreover the above-mentioned influences were all at work during the years 1850 and 1875, at work probably in a proportionately greater degree than during the last twelve years, and still they did not then produce a general fall in prices!

Repulsed on this ground our opponents retire behind the general assertion that what we are suffering from is: "general overproduction," to which some add over-population. What the great teacher of economic orthodoxy, J. S. Mill, declared to be "a theory essentially self-contradictory,"[1] is gravely put forward as a cause and an explanation. We have never seen any figures of the increase in stock, which seem to us in the least sufficient to account for the fall in prices that has taken place, but we will not examine this matter in detail. A broader statement of this theory will suffice to show its indefensibility. We are asked by such authorities as Mr. Hansard[2] and Mr. Fowler,[3] to believe that because the fruits of the earth have multiplied, because science has increased the power of man over nature, of mind over matter, thousands of our fellow men are prevented from earning enough to keep body and soul together. We are asked

---

[1] *Principles of Political Economy*, iii., 14.

[2] *Journal Institute of Bankers*, January, 1885.

[3] *Journal Institute of Bankers*, January, 1886.

to believe that part of the people are in want, because there is more wheat and more meat to consume, and that they are suffering from cold, because the production of coal has increased. Where the argument of overpopulation is added, the assertions become still more wonderful. For there we are invited to think that the remedy against this "too much of everything"[1] would be a decrease of population, *i.e.*, a reduction of the number of consumers. We refuse to believe any such doctrines. To do so would, in our opinion, involve the acknowledgment that what the world calls progress and civilization is a gross illusion; that the whole system of our capitalistic production has hopelessly broken down, and that if mankind is to be saved it must be on some new economic principles. Already do the socialists declare their readiness to take over the inheritance of a bankrupt society,[2] and certainly if we adopted the theory of our opponents we should have great difficulty in proving our economic solvency.

Our readers have now before them not only our own case, but also the objections raised against it as well as the alternative theory of the mono-metallists, and we hope we have succeeded in showing that their objections are not valid, and that the competing theory, as their own authority states, is " self-contradictory."

[1] *Economist*, 21st February, 1885.

[2] " A system of society, which piles up riches for the few at the cost of overwork, misery, and uncertainty for the many."—Hyndman, *Nineteenth Century*, 1885.

We therefore think ourselves justified in assuming our contentions to be proved. We are suffering from a crisis of low prices, but low prices which do not, looked upon as a whole, indicate real cheapness, which do not therefore promote increased consumption and thus bring about their own remedy, but low prices which are simply the expression of an increased and ever increasing purchasing power of gold. There is no want of production, there is no want of would be consumers, but the latter lack the means of getting command over the former. The wheels of commerce are revolving with slackened velocity owing to the disturbing element of an appreciating standard. Hence the helpless state into which trade has fallen, the absence of any tangible improvement, after years of watching and waiting !

The theory of gold appreciation consequent on the demonetization of silver being thus capable of exact demonstration has found numerous and able champions. Prominent among these are Mr. Goschen and Mr. Giffen. As these two gentlemen have so far declined to plead for the only remedy which to us seems logical and efficacious, we will now briefly examine the positions which they have taken up.

Mr. Goschen[1] admits, so far as we understand him, all the more important of our contentions. He looks upon the difficulties, however, as only passing. After a period of transition, the painful process of reduction of prices will come to an end, and things will adjust

[1] *Journal of Institute of Bankers*, May, 1883.

themselves on a new basis. Mr. Goschen is without doubt right. The only question is when this new level will be reached. Such a period of transition has in former epochs of our history lasted several hundred years. If we remember that, hitherto, Germany alone has sold silver, that, if the anti-silver crusade continues, other nations will have to follow her example, and that the silver of France, Holland and the United States[1] will then come on the market, when we try to estimate the period that must elapse before such operations can be carried through, and to picture the economic up-heavals which must result from them—upheavals which would include the *bankruptcy of the Indian Govern-ment*—it is clear that we are only at the beginning and not at the end of our difficulties.[2] We therefore can with absolute safety venture on the prophecy, that the

[1] To which list the name of India may, perhaps, have to be added. The following remarks of Mr. Goschen prove that he foresees what calamities such events would produce, but unless he is prepared to more boldly face the difficulties, his warnings will not be heeded . " A campaign against silver would be extremely dangerous even for countries with a gold standard." Again : "If other States were to carry on a propaganda in favor of a gold standard and the demone-tization of silver, the Indian Government would be obliged to reconsider its position, and might be forced to take measures similar to those taken elsewhere. In that case a scramble to get rid of silver might produce one of the greatest crises ever undergone by commerce."

[2] Those who advocate to let silver alone till it has reached its "natural price" would do well to consider that every further legal demonetization of silver lowers this "natural price," which, in fact, only exists in the brains of some theorists.

present generation will not live to see Mr. Goschen's readjusted commercial equilibrium. It will, however, be small consolation to the living generation of productive toilers to know that after they have come to grief and passed away in despair their successors will one day find a new and secure basis for trade, and Mr. Goschen must pardon them if they decline to await patiently their doom because statesmen find inaction safer and easier to advise than action.

Mr. R. Giffen has also come prominently before the public with his remarks upon the currency question, to which he has contributed some very valuable statistical data, showing the extent of the appreciation of gold. He appears to have somewhat modified his position towards the silver question once or twice, but he has never doubted the great influence of the demonetization of silver on the value of gold, and in one of his latest utterances, he is still distinctly of the opinion that " the recent course of prices, is the result in part of the diminished production of, and the increased extraordinary demand upon, the supply of gold."[1] But after going thus far Mr. Giffen stops. He looks upon the whole phenomenon as a most interesting one to study, a very proper one to explain, but one of which people with fixed incomes have no cause to complain, and to which mankind in general would do well to submit as it does to a thunderstorm or an earthquake.

[1] *Essays in Finance,* 1886.

There are, however, economists who will not yield without an effort at resistance, to this ever growing monetary difficulty, although, as the cause is not always correctly understood, the remedy proposed by them is not always the right one. Some propose to revive England's prosperity by altering her fiscal policy, by advocating the abandonment of free trade in favor of fair trade or protection. They overlook the fact that the depression we suffer from is, like its cause, world-wide and that though a duty on corn would somewhat improve the condition of agriculture, it would do so only temporarily, *i.e.*, as long as the fall in the price of silver has not outstripped the duty. Others hope to revive commerce by opening up new markets, trading which, as we said above, unless it brought new supplies of gold, would increase the demand on bullion and, therefore, still further depress prices. Others advocate the issue of £1 notes[1] as likely to reduce the pressure on gold, a palliative which could act only locally and which might render the English note issue less secure by increasing the superstructure of credit without increasing the foundation, and which, moreover, would not touch the root of the evil, the price of silver. Others venture to go further and advocate the issue of £1 notes against silver bullion[2] at market prices, a policy which would expose England to difficulties

[1] Mr. Ch. Gairdner, *l. c.*
[2] Lord Grey, letters to *Times*, February, 1886.

similar to those experienced in the United States
through the operation of the Bland Act.

But there is a school undoubtedly growing in influence and importance as the economic distress and
suffering of the world increase which having, as they
are convinced, discovered the source of the suffering
which commerce has undergone these last 12 years, are
prepared boldly to face the difficulty. Persuaded that
the social and commercial disturbances through which
we are passing and the still greater disturbances with
which we are threatened are the consequences of the
law of man and not of a law of nature, they demand of
legislation to restore what legislation has disturbed.
They demand the rehabilitation of silver.

This could of course be accomplished by going back
to the condition of things existing prior to 1872, by
inducing Germany to adopt silver mono-metallism, and
France the double standard, but people acquainted
with the condition of contemporary politics know this
to be an impossible demand. To day, if silver is to be
rehabilitated by European powers, it can only be done
by an international agreement which would open the
mints of all the important states to the free coinage of
both gold and silver at a fixed ratio. No half-hearted
measures with all their attendant evils ; no limited
coinage like that under the Bland Bill; no issuing of
" grey notes " at ever varying market prices, full and
complete admission of silver as a legal tender; such is

the aim and the demand of the bi-metallists. By this means the former equilibrium of commerce will be brought back, the dislocated par between gold and silver will be restored, the fall in prices, so far as it is a result of the decline in the value of silver, will be arrested and the ultimate cause of the present economic crisis will be reached. The greatest and most important branch of the world's commerce, the exchange of the productions of the East and of the West, would again be placed on a firm footing, and while Europe and America would enjoy the benefit of stable prices, the people and the government of India would be freed from their greatest financial, and therefore potentially political danger,[1] the loss on exchange. The nightmare of our opponents, the alleged overproduction, would disappear as if by magic, not by artificially curtailing the supplies but in the only satisfactory manner, by the increase of consumption, by the restored ability of the masses to absorb what is or ought to be produced, not for the benefit of the favored few, but to the advantage of the great body of the people.

Bi-metallism is not,—as the reader who has followed our reasoning will understand—a specious device to make the world happy by issuing more money;

[1] " Our financial position is affected from day to day by the continuous fall in the value of exchange. This state of affairs would be an evil of the greatest magnitude in any country in the world, in a country such as India, *it is pregnant with danger.*"—*Despatch of Government of India,* 2nd February, 1886.

D

it is a means to prevent the economic condition of the
world from being disturbed by a wanton interference
with monetary laws. Bi-metallists know very well
that in one sense there exists always enough money ;
that money, like water, will ever find its own level ;
but they reckon up the economic cost of lowering that
level so as to be able to do without silver, and wish to
preserve the world by timely measures from the dangers
and the suffering attending such an operation.

It is not so long ago since bi-metallists were regarded
in England as people with whom to argue was condescen-
sion. Newspapers jealous of their economic reputation
would refuse to open their columns to statements from
such sources.[1] The new doctrine could not be found in
any of the classic text books of political economy,
written mostly before this currency difficulty arose ; it
was therefore not acceptable to that great majority of
so-called thinkers who prefer to adopt the conclusions
of others to investigating themselves how far these conclusions are still applicable under the changed conditions
of economic life. But suffering is a grand teacher, and
bi-metallism is now becoming so strong that it is met
no longer with contempt but by arguments, which we
hold we can do no better than detail and carefully

[1] Of the Metropolitan Press only the *Bullionist* has from the first
embraced the people's cause in this question. More recently the
World, too, has fought with ability and intelligence for a principle
which a larger but less sensible world will have to accept sooner or
later.

examine. Here is a list of the objections, which the more enlightened of our opponents have raised against us, and which are supposed to dispose of the claim of bi-metallism to be a scientific and practical solution of our difficulties.

The first is a preliminary objecton raised by Mr. Giffen "that it does not come within the functions of a government to settle such questions as are intended to be settled by international bi-metallism."[1] The answer to this objection is complete and very simple. Not only have nearly all thinkers of mankind, from the time of Aristotle down to our own day, maintained that governments should possess a supreme control over money and currency, not only have governments exercised these powers, nay, if philosophers and history were as much against us, as they are unquestionably in our favor, we should still claim this very authority as belonging to the state, for the state must have the right of interference wherever the well-being of its citizens is in question. This right has on previous occasions been exercised by Parliament in England, and whether it is to be again so exercised is simply a question "of monetary expediency."[2] The point will become clear beyond a doubt by assuming an extreme case. Supposing that

[1] *On some bi-metallic fallacies.—Journal of Institute of Bankers,* June, 1886.

[2] Even the *Economist* was therefore obliged to admit that it was "unable to say that Mr. Giffen succeeded in proving this part of his case."—22nd May, 1886.

instead of an appreciation of gold of 25 or 35 % we had experienced a depreciation of that metal, and a very great depreciation. Supposing that from some cause or other gold had become exceedingly abundant, and 1000 sovereigns had fallen to the value of 1000 pence. Would the officials receiving their salaries on the old scale then come before the public and declare that on principles of metaphysics government is not to interfere!

An objection that goes to the very root of this question is that bi-metallism would alter the legal definition of the Pound Sterling. The answer to the old historic and familiar question " *What is a pound?* " would have to be modified. This is quite true. But the answer to this question has varied frequently and considerably in English history, and the present reply that a pound is 123·274 grains gold 11/12 fine has been the law of the land for barely three generations. England has been in turn bi-metallic, silver mono-metallic and gold mono-metallic. Moreover, although ever since 1816 the answer to the above question has nominally remained the same, it is proved beyond cavil that, as a matter of fact, during the last 12 years the meaning of this answer has been considerably altered, for the events above referred to have had the effect of virtually making the sovereign heavier than it was. The real question for parliament is which is preferable; to alter the words of the statute so as to make them conform to the actual facts of life, or to ignore these facts, to take one's stand on strict legality, and let the world take care of itself on the old maxim: *Fiat justitia pereat mundus.* We think there can be but little doubt as to the answer to be given to this question. For statesmen exist to make and to remake laws as the everchanging conditions of human existence require.

But it is said that it would be monstrous folly to change a standard to which England owes some of the most prosperous periods of her history. This is the old fallacy of *post hoc, ergo propter hoc,* as Lord Beaconsfield perceived already when he said : " It is the greatest delusion in the world to attribute the commercial preponderance and prosperity of England to our having a gold standard." [1] The fact is the British Empire prospered under the quixotic system of having two different standards so long as France was good enough to be the reservoir which kept them at a steady level.[2] Since France has ceased to perform this function England's prosperity has declined, her manufacturers are suffering, and her trade has ceased to expand. Clearly the time has arrived for English statesmen to think of securing by their own action those benefits for their country which it formerly enjoyed through the bi-metallic system of the Latin Union.

[1] Speech at Glasgow, November 6th, 1873.

[2] Moreover, during some of the most prosperous periods of her history England was bi-metallic.

Another objection which is based on principles of strict legality is that bi-metallism would be a "breach of faith." "Payments which have been stipulated for in gold cannot be allowed to be made in silver." The question is whether repayments under the present ever-appreciating standard are not in truth a greater injustice to the debtor than repayments under the bi-metallic system would be to the creditor. In support of an affirmative answer to this question it could be urged that up to 1873 the English standard, though nominally gold mono-metallic, was in effect "vicariously bi-metallic."[1] But we think the whole objection would have little practical significance were once bi-metallism introduced, because whatever be the ratio adopted between gold and silver, the two metals would be at par, and there would be no difference in the value of the coins of the same denomination whether of one metal or the other.

Another objection frequently raised against bi-metallism, is that it would be a new form of inflation. It is alleged that what bi-metallists aim at is simply more money, that consequently the difference between their system and inflation is only one of degree not of kind. But bi-metallists merely want to prevent the entire and complete destruction of the existing level of prices with

[1] Through France. As to the manner in which one country can bestow upon another the advantages of bi-metallism, see D. Barbour: *Theory of Bi-metallism*, xii.

its train of untold misery. The total abandonment of silver would be an immense monetary and social revolution needlessly brought about by some interested or foolish theorists. Against this danger bi-metallism provides a preserving and conservative policy. We frankly admit that such a policy would be accompanied by a rise in the prices of some commodities from the present low level, but wherever such is the case it would only be a part-restoration of previous quotations. Such a result is so totally different from inflation, that it is difficult always to believe in the *bonâ fide* ignorance of those who make the above charge.

But even the admission that some prices would again be raised if silver were rehabilitated is fastened upon by our opponents as an argument against bi-metallism. For is it not clear that producers would thereby be robbed of the cheapness of some raw materials enjoyed at present! Would the labourer not be deprived of his cheap loaf? As to the labouring classes we have already discussed the question of their prosperity under the present economic conditions, and commented also on the peculiarity of this zeal for their well-being exhibited by the capitalistic mono-metallists, and we are quite prepared to take their own answer to the question of which is preferable, prosperity and higher prices, or cheap bread and no work.[1] But as to destroying the

---

[1] We believe in high prices of labor as being not only a proof, but a cause of prosperity. Our opponents worship low prices and labor

cheapness of raw materials it is evident that bi-metallism could not do that where the cheapness is "real," is the result of the "ingenuity of man." It would, however, do so where cheapness is only apparent, where it is merely the expression of the appreciation of gold. But this, instead of being an evil, we look upon as a blessing. Moreover, it is a fact well known to those who have studied the history of prices,[1] that there is always less fear of a rise in prices through an increase of currency, than of a fall in prices through a contraction of money, because an augmented circulation is always accompanied by a growth of trade which quickly absorbs the new supplies of money.

We now come to the objection which is supposed to be the *reductio ad absurdum* of bi-metallism. If the addition of silver (so it runs) to gold as money is productive of all the advantages here set forth, the further addition of copper and iron, etc., should, on the same grounds, increase still further the general weal of humanity.[2] Bi-metallism is therefore reproached with

so cheap that working people just earn enough to pay interest to money lenders and taxes to Government. A one-sided creditor policy has more than once in history produced unpleasant results, when the quiet of Statesmen was interrupted by the trumpet call of revolution.

[1] Tooke and Newmarch, *History of Prices.*

[2] " What bi-metallists claim is practically protection for silver in the principal markets of the world; and if for silver, why not for copper and pig-iron ? "—Speech of Mr. Harvey, *Journal Institute of Bankers*, June, 1886.

demanding either *too much* or else *not enough*. We will not linger to expose the fallacy of such reasoning. In claiming the rehabilitation of silver, we ask for a return to a former social status, a status on which most of our social relations are based, and which it would cause untold misery to totally destroy. What we advocate is a policy of true conservatism. If our recommendations went beyond what is here proposed, we should plead for as great a social revolution—though in the opposite direction—as that which the demonetization of silver will bring about. None of our arguments for bi-metallism would apply to a system of currency which embraces more than what has been money ever since the dawn of history—silver and gold.

A very short-sighted objection is that silver is too heavy for a standard metal. For many transactions of daily life silver is better suited than gold. As to the larger banking transactions they are carried on by cheques or notes, and gold would be practically as inconvenient for them as silver.[1] The daily transactions of Lombard Street can only be got through with " representative " money.

A favourite theory of mono-metallists is that gold is

---

[1] " The only objection to the use of silver as the standard is its bulk, which renders it unfit for the large payments required in a wealthy country, but this objection is entirely removed by the substituting of a paper money as the general circulating medium of the country."—D. Ricardo, *Proposals for an economical and secure currency.*

by nature the standard of rich and silver that of poor
nations. It is difficult to see how on this theory the
general introduction of bi-metallism can be objected to.
For under the double standard the precious metals
would have free scope to distribute themselves in the
most automatic manner to the needs of the different
nations. For all that, as Mr. Barbour correctly says,
the above theory of first and second class nations, is
absurd. For what should happen if all nations became
equally rich ? And who will decide whether a nation
be rich or poor ?

The objection to silver as money, that it is less
suited because less stable in value though often heard,
reposes on a complete want of a comprehension of facts.
Measured in the only correct manner, *i.e.*, by its purchasing power, silver has been more stable than gold ever
since its so-called depreciation began. As to the London market price of silver, though it has varied largely
it has only done so in exact proportion to the Bombay
or Calcutta market price of gold.

It is further objected that the rise in the price of
silver consequent on the introduction of bi-metallism,
would give such a stimulus to its production, that the
world would soon be inundated with the white metal,
and that consequently prices would rise enormously.
This purely theoretical reasoning assumes that the
production of the precious metals is subject to the same
economic laws as the productions of other commodities.

This is, however, not the case. The production of the precious metals depends more or less on chance. Besides, the gambling spirit of man is so large a factor in gold and silver mining that it is carried on without much reference to the value of the product.[1] The history of the last 12 years proves the correctness of this view. During this period silver has heavily declined in price, while gold has appreciated. If our opponents were right the production of silver should have decreased, that of gold augmented. The very reverse has happened. There may, of course, be here and there a silver mine which will be shut up should the price of silver fall much more, but it would be a very long time before the total production was thereby affected. Moreover in many mines silver is a bye-product. The same causes, however, that prevent the fall in the price of silver, from producing a decrease in its production, will prevent its rise from being followed by any material increase.

The objection diametrically opposed to the last is that of Mr. Giffen. Mr. Giffen is not afraid of too great a rise in prices. His objection is that "assuming the bi-metallic scheme to be successful, gold and silver being equalized, the future course of prices will be regulated by the aggregate annual production not of the one

---

[1] " Even in California, the richest of all gold countries, gold was produced, on the average, at a loss ; in Nevada, the richest of silver countries, silver was produced, on an average, at a loss."—A. Del Mar, *Money in Civilization.*

metal but of the two. The proportion of that annual production to the stocks of the two metals in use, would, however, be much the same as the proportion of the production of the one metal to the stock of that metal only. The future course of prices would therefore be much the same, whether bi-metallism be adopted or not." [1] The same reasoning underlies Mr. Giffen's third point in his essay on "Some bi-metallic fallacies," and in the discussion on that paper particular stress was laid on this argument by Professor Marshall who, however, qualified it by adding " except so far as the bi-metallists have reasons for knowing that the silver mines will yield their produce more steadily than the gold mines."[2] Now, as a matter of fact, bi-metallists have reasons for anticipating a more steady yield of the silver, than of the gold mines, for history teaches this to have been the case in the past, and Professor Süss[3] proves that it will be so in the future, and it is difficult to understand why mono-metallists have not been able to get hold of the same facts. As to the above objection itself, it is, as we said, the exact opposite to that we have just considered, and we might fairly leave these two classes of opponents to settle this difference between themselves. We will not, however, shield ourselves behind such technicalities but will examine this statement on its merits. Undoubtedly

[1] *Essays in Finance*, 1886.

[2] *Journal of Institute of Bankers*, June, 1886.

[3] *Die Zukunft des Goldes*, Vienna, 1877.

it affords us one consolation, inasmuch as it admits bi-
metallism to be of some good,[1] though it contends that
this good would only be temporary. But even this last
contention reposes on an error which our readers will probably have already perceived. Like one of the objections
against the theory of gold appreciation that we have
already examined, it rests entirely upon the *Quantitäts-
Theorie* and takes no account of the influence of the
present depreciation of silver or the prices in the gold
countries. But what we are suffering from, we again
repeat, is not so much the insufficiency of gold, as the
fall in the value of silver which, as we have shown, is
unsettling trade and contracts all the world over. Bi-
metallism would remedy this fall, and remedy it once
for all, and constitute, therefore, a real and permanent
cure against a general fall in prices such as the present
generation has witnessed. The hair-splitting specula-
tions of Mr. Giffen and Professor Marshall may therefore
be summarily dismissed.

The last objection against bi-metallism which we propose to consider, is the one most frequently raised. It
is to be found not only in popular authors, such as J. S.
Mill,[2] but also in the writings of exact thinkers such as
J. Locke[3] and K. Marx.[4] This objection is that "it is

[1] "The question then is not whether bi-metallism would do some
good : that is granted."—Speech of Professor Marshall, *l. c.*

[2] *Principles of Political Economy*, iii., 10.

[3] *Considerations of the lowering of interest.*

[4] *Das Kapital*, I., 3.

impossible to have two measures of value." [1]   But it is overlooked that under a bi-metallic system there would only be *one* measure of value, *viz.* : gold and silver held together in a fixed ratio.   In favour of our opponents it is asserted, that the money of a bi-metallic country never really consists of both metals, but of one only, the " least valuable," that instead of there being a " double " there is therefore in fact only an " alternative " standard. To this we reply that though the circulation of a bi-metallic country may vary between gold and silver, the standard remains invariable.   This important distinction between standard and circulation will remove the misconceptions, and disposes of the objection.

We have so far vindicated the correctness of the bi-metallic principles in an indirect way, by refuting the arguments brought forward against it.   There is, however, one point in connexion with bi-metallism, for which indirect proof does not suffice and which must be faced in the most direct way possible.   This is the question : Can a ratio of exchange be fixed between gold and silver by legislative enactments ? or to put it differently : Is it possible to keep gold and silver at par at the legal ratio by simply opening the mints to the free coinage of both metals over a sufficiently large

---

[1] In the *Physics and Metaphysics of Money* of R. Gibbons, this objection takes the following neat form : " The double standard is as much of a solecism as a double single, it implies that one and one do not make two, and that things which are not equal to the same may be equal to one another."   Comment is unnecessary.

area? Upon the answer to this question depends the decision whether ultimately bi-metallism forms a scientific solution of the currency question or not. Here is, as Professor Nicholson says, the central point around which "the battle of the standard" most hotly rages.

History tells us that the ratio between gold and silver has fluctuated a good deal. Superficial students have from these facts drawn the conclusion that it would be impossible to fix such a ratio by law. But a closer study of history reveals the fact that the fluctuations which occurred in the ratio were the result of the legislative enactments of the nation, which for the time being controlled the principal supplies of the two metals. At whatever ratio such a nation coined silver and gold, that ratio became the basis of the relative value of these metals.[1] Countries of less economic power had either to conform to that ratio or to submit to see that metal which they undervalued, and which in the open market would therefore command a higher price and be called the "dearer metal," disappear from circula-

[1] Mr. A. Del Mar, in his letter to Lord Iddesleigh, has pointed out that the ratio between the two metals has always been fixed for the advantage of the nation fixing it, that when gold was the greater product of such a nation it raised the value of gold, and when silver became its greater product it raised the value of silver. Thus the more plentiful metal produced or controlled by the nation altering the ratio was always the metal that was raised in value. Political Economy tries to disseminate the doctrine that the ratio is governed by the relative quantities of metal produced, while, *de facto*, it is rather governed by the opposite principle.

tion, in accordance with what is known as the " Gresham
.law."

It will be noticed that in thus speaking of the causes
of the relative value of gold and silver, we have considered neither the cost of production nor the com-.,
mercial demand for consumption in the arts, &c. The
reason for this is that in determining the value of the
precious metals the mint demand is the all powerful
factor. No doubt these metals would possess a certain,
possibly a high, value even if none were coined, but the
constant demand induced by the fact that the mints
are open to coin any quantity into legal tender forms
after all the main feature that decides their value.
" The artificial value of gold and silver is much greater
than the real."[1] This is why by the control of the
former we can control the price, and why by determining the ratio between the artificial value of gold and
silver (*i.e.* the ratio at which the mints are·open) we are
able to fix practically the relative value of gold and
silver.

It is necessary to point out here that bi-metallism
does not attempt to actually fix the value of gold and
silver, it does not even attempt to fix the relative values
of these metals, all it does is to create a demand for
these metals at the legal ratio. Bi-metallism is not,

---

[1] " Mankind having consented to put *an imaginary value* upon gold
and silver, have made them the common pledges."—J. Locke, *Considerations on the lowering of interest.*

therefore, opposed to the laws of supply and demand, nor does it in any way interfere with them; on the contrary it is based upon those laws.[1] Of course it is clear that the greater the number of the mints open to the free coinage of gold and silver, the greater will be the demand for these metals at the legal ratio, the greater therefore the minuteness with which this ratio will be maintained. But should by any chance the market prices of the two metals deviate from the fixed legal ratio there will at once arise an increased demand for the cheaper metal which will continue till the legal and the market ratio are again identical. Through this " compensatory action," bi-metallism secures in an automatic manner the constant equilibrium between the two metals at the legal rates.

We therefore find that law can fix a ratio between gold and silver, and can under certain conditions strictly maintain this ratio. Of course there is a limit to the choice of the ratio, and this limit finds its scientific expression in the following formula : " The relation of value of the two metals both being money, must be between the relations of value they would have to one another, if each were exclusively money."[2] What these

---

[1] " It is a mistake to suppose that the bi-metallists wish to see a law passed which shall fix the market price of gold and silver. Under the bi-metallic system the State simply undertakes to coin both gold and silver freely if brought to it."—D. Barbour, *Theory of Bi-metallism*, VIII.

[2] On the above formula depends the answer to the question which

E

limits really are we do not profess to know nor do we think it profitable to speculate concerning them. As the monetary value of gold and silver largely exceeds their commercial value, it is quite clear that these limits are very wide and that not only the present ratio of 1:22 but also the old ratio of 1:15½ falls within them.

It is asserted, however, by our opponents that whatever be the ratio adopted it is possible that should the silver mines become very rich and the gold mines exhausted, the two metals could not be kept in circulation together though the ratio might be maintained. Gold would practically disappear. Everybody will grant that with the present stock of gold in the world there is exceedingly small probability of such a contingency happening. Still if asked whether such an event is absolutely beyond the range of possibility, we should reply in the negative. But in spite of the apparent far-sightedness of this objection, we cannot congratulate those, who, like Professor Marshall[1] have raised it, on their perspicacity. For if gold should ever become so scarce, that under a bi-metallic system it would disappear, the countries that do not possess a bi-metallic

is often regarded as a *reductio ad absurdum* of bi-metallism, whether a ratio of 1:1 could be established by law. That such a ratio is practically not desirable, because it would produce in an opposite direction the evils of a dislocated par of exchange between East and West, the intelligent reader need not be told.

[1] "We think that gold will practically go out."—*Journal of Institute of Bankers*, June, 1886.

standard but adhere to the single gold valuation would be in a sorry plight indeed. They would undergo a social revolution in comparison to which the wildest schemes of confiscation proposed by the most fanatic section of the socialistic and nihilistic party fade into utter insignificance. Even the most distant chance of such an occurrence would make bi-metallism a veritable saviour of society, a measure on which, to speak the language of the learned professor, a difference of opinion "as to quantity of its effects " would no longer be possible. The condition of society would then be such that the following words of the American legislators would but understate the case.[1]   " Should the world come to the gold unit as the sole legal tender, that metal might become so valuable as compared with other commodities and so scarce in proportion to the enormous demands made upon it, that the money barons of this and other countries controlling a few hundred millions of gold, might control the destines of nations and absolutely dominate the welfare of mankind."

But besides the theoretical demonstration that it would be possible to keep the ratio between gold and silver constant by law we have actual historic experience of legislation having thus controlled the market price. From the beginning of this century to the year 1872 the bi-metallic standard of France and the countries of

---

[1] *Minority Report of the Committee on Coinage, Weights and Measures —House of Representatives*, Washington, February, 1886.

the Latin Union kept the ratio of gold and silver at
1:15½. As these countries were surrounded by both
silver and gold mono-metallic nations the demands for
remittances one way or the other from time to time
slightly altered this proportion. The exchange between
gold and silver consequently fluctuated between the two
" specie points " just as does the exchange between
London and Melbourne. But to draw, as Mr. Giffen
has done,[1] from these fluctuations the conclusion that
France failed to maintain the ratio, is as logical as it
would be to say that a sovereign ceases to be a sovereign
when cheques in London are quoted in Melbourne at 3%
premium. As a matter of fact during all these years
France under most difficult circumstances maintained
the ratio, not alone for herself but for the whole world.
Mr. D. Barbour shows this clearly enough, and we will
conclude this part of our subject with his remark :
" To contend in face of the facts stated that the legal
ratio fixed under the bi-metallic system between gold
and silver when used as money will not control and
regulate the market price of the two metals is simply to
abandon reason, argument and experience, and take
refuge in assertion."[2]

We have finished our main task. We have demonstrated the connexion between the fall in silver and the
appreciation of gold and the commercial and social disturbances, which are the characteristics of our times.

[1] *On some bi-metallic fallacies.* Point 2.—*Journal of Institute of
Bankers,* June, 1886.

[2] *Theory of Bi-metallism,* XIII.

We have shown that the policy of waiting on events pursued hitherto will never bring about a settlement and that if things are allowed to drift in the future as they have done in the past the state of trade and the condition of the people must go from bad to worse, though a temporary recovery of silver may afford passing relief and kindle false hopes.[1]   We have pointed out that for silver there exists no fixed " natural price " and that to found a policy on the expectation that such could be reached is like hunting a shadow.   We have also endeavoured to prove that there is a remedy for the abnormal condition into which we have fallen, that the reinstatement and rehabilitation of silver by the establishment of a bi-metallic system of money would afford the much desired relief once and for all, and that such a system is possible.

But we must not yet lay down our pen.   In a case like ours it is not sufficient to propound a theory and to establish its scientifie claims.   As practical men of business we have to examine into the means of carrying the theory into practice, and into the chances of such a consummation being reached.   With this two-fold investigation will conclude our remarks.

[1] The recovery in the quotation of silver which took place on the announcement of|the appointment of a Royal Commission "To enquire into the recent changes in the relative values of the precious metals " is a remarkable proof that the price of silver depends not on cost of production or any of the other causes alleged by mono-metallists, but on legislation, and on hopes and fears of legislation.   Should the Royal Commission disappoint such hopes or fears, the price of silver would probably again resume its downward march.

We have seen above that the larger the area over which bi-metallism is established the more certain will be the maintenance of the legal ratio. The most zealous, the most enlightened champions of bi-metallism advocate therefore the establishment by international treaty of a great Bi-metallic Union of which all the principal European Powers as well as the United States of America would form part. With the mints of all these countries open to the free coinage of both silver and gold at the same ratio it is admitted even by the nestor of gold mono-metallism, Professor Soetbeer[1] that it would be impossible for the market prices of the precious metals to deviate from their mint prices.

There can be no doubt that such a union would be the best and the most satisfactory solution of the silver difficulty and of that whole group of questions which cluster around it. Its establishment therefore should be the ultimate aim of the exertions of all bi-metallists some of whom, like Mr. Cernuschi, and the late Mr. E. Seyd, by their constant efforts in this direction may lay claim to the title of true philanthropists.

Unfortunately this most comprehensive solution of our troubles is probably the most difficult to bring about, for the fact that it presupposes an international agreement

[1] "If all commercial states, without exception, in law and practice adopt and maintain the bi-metallic standard at one ratio for their entire coinage, with unconditional freedom of coinage of both worlds, it cannot be denied that in such a case, for the present, and probably for a long period to come, a permanent and stable relation between gold and silver will be secured."—*Letter to Neue Freie Presse of Vienna*, 10th October, 1876.

opens to our opponents quite a new vista of objections, of which they have availed themselves to the full. If the whole truth could be known it would probably be seen that it is to their objections against such an agreement that they largely owe the success which so far has attended their obstructive efforts. The soundness of the bi-metallic theory is conceded, the power of the law to keep gold and silver at par at the legal ratio by simply operating through the ordinary laws of supply and demand is admitted, but it is objected that the State should never enter into an international treaty about the standard, because it must not bargain away its absolute freedom in the exercise of one of its most vital sovereign rights, that of money. Moreover treaties have been broken before and may be broken again, and it is sarcastically asked whether in such a case a country should enforce the bi-metallic stipulations at the point of the sword. The difficulties that have arisen in connexion with the Latin Monetary Union are cited as a lesson and a warning.[1]

[1] It is with arguments of the above kind that the German government have so far resisted the demands of the German bi-metallists. In his celebrated speech of the 22nd January, 1886, Herr von Scholz, Prussian Minister of Finance, after a confused reference to the legal tender silver of France, Germany and Holland, strongly accentuated the difficulties of an international bi-metallic agreement in an age of national armies when war was not yet abolished. He warned his hearers against infusing by treaty blood into their economic body which could fulfil the functions of blood only under certain condition, and which might remain in that body an obstacle, and not help, to its growth when these conditions ceased to exist, *i.e.*, after the treaty was torn.

These objections sound well, and look statesmen-like and patriotic, but for all that we think we shall be able to show that they are shallow and inadequate. A really national currency, absolute and true monetary independence, exists only in those countries that have a numerary system, *i.e.*, among modern States only in those with an inconvertible paper money; States scarcely to be regarded as models of finance. All other countries, among them the economically strongest, possess a commodity money and therefore depend for their supplies on the existing stocks and the production of that commodity of which their money consists. The larger the existing quantity of that money commodity the less will be the chance of financial disturbance through the action of the currency, and this is a reason for preferring the double standard to one consisting of either metal only, apart from all the social considerations upon which we have laid so much stress.

But whatever be the money commodity adopted, every country that possesses a commodity money depends as to the value of that money upon what happens to that commodity anywhere in the world. To speak under these circumstances about the absolute freedom enjoyed by a government with regard to its standard is absurd. The demonetization, for instance, of silver by Germany took place without England or any other country having been consulted. Still it is beyond doubt that no event of recent times has had so important a bearing on the domestic history and the economic development of England or so revolutionary an effect on the Imperial relations of England and India as this legislation. And where is the monetary independence, the monetary autonomy of England and India to-day? Monetary independence indeed! People who are satisfied with words may think it exists; people who believe only in facts, know that it does not. We all remember the fluctuations of silver and Indian Exchange when the fate of the Bland Act was being discussed in America, how the currency of the Indian Empire went up and down as newspaper correspondents expressed this or that view of the chances of suspension or non-suspension of an American act of congress. And though it was nominally only the Indian currency that fluctuated, the reader who has followed us so far will know that in reality the stability of England's boasted standard was just as much affected.[1]

But if every state with a commodity money, *i.e.*, with a sound currency, as we call it, is at present *de facto* only enjoying a nominal control over its money, an international agreement which though tying the hands of a country would at the same time render the currency

---

[1] Should the Bland Bill really be repealed, the monetary autonomy (!) of England and India will be demonstrated in the most perfect manner possible. But the faith of the mono-metallists in their own theories is so great that we are quite prepared to believe that even the most violent monetary upheavals in London would not induce them to stir in this question convinced, as they apparently are, that such events are inseparable from true "independence."

more secure from the disturbances caused by the action
of other countries, seems to us to enlarge rather than
contract the sovereign rights of a government. We are
therefore distinctly of the opinion that if an international agreement on the ratio of gold and silver is
being concluded it would be far better for the British
Empire to participate, and have a voice, in the delibera-
tion than to remain outside and let others decide the
fate of the two metals which form the basis of her two
separate standards.

Of course such a treaty could be broken. Nobody will
deny this possibility. But our opponents have, so far,
never given any tangible reason for such a step, though
with most of them reasons are as plentiful as black-
berries.' Nor can a satisfactory motive be suggested.
So long as both metals kept at par everybody would
be satisfied and no inducement would exist to bring back
again the present difficulties which experience has shown
fall on all alike and which no nation can so control as to
contrive its own safe escape. And as long as no violation
of the treaty occurred both metals must keep at par.
Should war break out governments would be sufficiently
occupied with ensuring the maintenance of specie payments to think of discarding one of the metals.

As to the case of the Latin Union, instead of being
analogous, as alleged, it is rather a contrast to the
proposed Bi-metallic Union. The Latin Union provided for the coinage of identical pieces of money in

different countries with legal tender power throughout the Union.[1] All the difficulties that arose proceeded from this cause. No such dispute could arise under the proposed bi-metallic agreement, which extends only to the standard while each state would remain free to coin its own money which would have no legal tender power beyond the country of its origin.

But though it is, as we see, easy enough to refute all the arguments which are brought forward against an International Bi-metallic agreement, we fear that a dispassionate survey of the situation does not encourage the hope of such an agreement being established in the near future. France while accumulating and jealously guarding an ever increasing stock of gold is apathetic. The German government, endeavouring to imitate the action of France by also striving to get command over as much gold as possible and overlooking the internal social disorders, persuade themselves that as regards the currency question Germany is " in a relatively most favourable position"[2] and can afford to look on. In England the preponderance of official opinion is undoubtedly still under the influence of the gold mono-metallic teaching. Under these circumstances the enlightened statesmen and financiers of India remain preachers in the desert !

[1] Similar stipulations of the Vienna Mint Convention caused like difficulties between Austria and Germany, in consequence of which the latter country, when demonetizing silver, had to recognise its responsibility for the Austrian pieces of one and two Thalers coined under that convention prior to 1867.

[2] Speech of Finance Minister von Scholz in the Prussian *Landtag,* 22nd January, 1886.

Failing the international agreement, there is another
chance for bi-metallism which so far has not much
actuality, but which, should the fall of silver become
more pronounced, is likely to come to the front, *viz.*, an
Anglo-Indian double standard. The objections against
treaties with foreign powers would not apply to such an
agreement. Moreover, it is well-known that an international treaty has only a chance of being adopted
either on the French basis of 1:15½ or in the American
ratio of 1:16. Anglo-Indian bi-metallism on the other
hand could be established without any reference to these
historic relations and at a ratio nearer the present
market price of silver, say at 1:18 or 1:20. This would
be a recommendation of the scheme with those theorists
who are still in the thraldom of the notion of "natural
price." But it would also be supported by many business
men practically connected with the trade with the East.
For if there is one thing that many Anglo-Indian merchants fear almost as much as the fall of the rupee to 1/-,
it is its rise to the old 2/-, which would happen should
the 1:15½ ratio be stored with or without England.

We think these fears exaggerated. We concede
that part of the trade and manufactures which have
been built up in India during the last ten years
under the shadow of the low exchange might again
perish if exchange rises much, but we also believe
it will be but a small part. For, as we have previously
shown, the chief effect of the fall in exchange was the

fall in gold prices, the appreciation of gold, and therefore the chief effect of rise in exchange would be the restoration of gold prices, the fall of the purchasing power of gold to its former level.[1] But whether the above fears are well grounded or not, they exist, and so far as they exercise any influence it will, when the day of action arrives, be in favor of a ratio more advantageous to gold than 1:15½ or even 1:16. And the day of action may be nearer than is generally supposed.

In these days when the words "Imperial Federation" are assuming so large an influence; when the desire to weld the different component parts of the British Empire more closely together is making rapid advance, it cannot but strike thoughtful observers that there could be no greater barrier between England and her greatest dependency than the depreciation of silver, a barrier which is continually rising as silver falls in price. On the other hand nothing could, next to a common language, form a better means of cementing the union of all the subjects of the British crown, than a common standard of money.[2] To doubt that commercially the

[1] "The conclusion which is indicated from a consideration of all facts is that an increase in the rate of exchange would be accompanied by a corresponding rise in gold prices and no restriction of the Indian export trade would result from a recovery in the rate of exchange."—*Minute of Mr. J. E. O'Conor,* Simla, 13th July, 1886.

[2] After Prince Bismark had by the sword created the German Empire, one of his first steps of economic reform, to consolidate the new structure, was to propose a common standard. This is how statesmen understand "Federation."

first gold nation and the greatest silver country on earth could dictate to the world to-day the ratio of gold and silver would be to question the mercantile preponderance of Great Britain. The chances for such an agreement are therefore perhaps less remote than would at first appear. The Indian administrators have already emancipated themselves from the baneful influence of a few mistaken sentences of J. S. Mill. And it would be a libel on English statesmen to despair of their being roused in time to a clear perception of the danger ahead; to say that they would be unequal to the task of putting an end to that monstrous anomaly of two different standards under one crown without a connecting link between them ; and to assume that they would be unable to prevent the greatest empire of modern history from going a-wreck on the same rock on which the greatest Empire of the Old World went to pieces—the rock of monetary disorganization.

But even if England and India should fail to act, there is a hope of seeing the currency question settled in a manner which will frustrate the efforts of the capitalist classes to forge the golden chains wherewith to hold labor in bondage, and which will spare the world the dismal spectacle of the violent social upheavals otherwise unavoidable. We base this hope on the consideration of the influence—an influence which would be decisive in the " battle of the standards "—likely to be exercised by a nation with whom we have occupied ourselves thus far but cursorily, viz., the United States of America.

As the largest produce exporting country in the world the United States have a paramount interest in the stability of prices. The disorganization of the world's markets consequent on the fall of silver, though, as we have seen, felt all over the globe, is felt nowhere so severely as in America. Cheap silver enables and obliges India to compete at low prices, not only in the wheat markets, but in those for cotton, hides, linseed, and even wool, and the losses sustained by America through this competition are enormous.[1]   As a consequence the farming industries of the States are suffering acutely, and through them the whole economic body of the nation.

Against these losses America is unable to protect her farmers, as do France and Germany, by corn duties, for she is a food exporting country.   Against these losses, moreover, no compensating benefit can be named in America, such as the import of cheap bread which in England some economists persuade themselves is a sufficient set-off against the crying evils of gold appreciation.   Nor can these losses be ascribed to defective laws of real property, as they often are in Europe, where demagogues tell the people that agricultural distress is owing to " landlords " and to " rent."   In

---

[1] In a memorial to the United States Senate, by the Hon. J. P. Jones, the money loss to the United States on wheat and cotton, from Sept., 1885, to March, 1886, through competition of cheap silver is estimated at $125,000,000 to 150,000,000, and the loss of railway traffic thereby caused at $15,000,000 to 17,000,000.

America the evil is seen, if not understood, in all its nakedness, and the connexion between the price of silver and the prosperity of the country is widely recognized.[1] American statesmen and legislators have therefore never really been misled by the clamour of the gold mono-metallists. The financial history of their country has supplied them with too many practical lessons not to make them proof against the declarations of mere theorists. Of course there exists in the United States a gold party consisting principally of the National Banking interests and the foreign mercantile community in New York and the stock exchange connexions in the East; but though that party has command over large means and greatly influences the Eastern press, it has never yet succeeded in imposing its views on Congress.

Consequently when that party desired to change the metallic standard of the country from gold and silver to gold only, it was surreptitiously[2] done, not by passing a

[1] When we drew attention in the "Future of Silver" (*Journal Institute of Bankers*, April, 1885,) to the fact that the Bland Bill is of vital importance to the farmers of the United States, the *Economist*, (21st March, 1885,) in a captious article remarked : "that it is worthy of note that this is not understood where it is most necessary, namely, by the Americans themselves." A legion of newspaper articles, as well as numberless speeches of representative men in America during the last year testify to a full comprehension of this question by the Americans.

[2] "The act when passed was not real except by title." "The ancient money of the country was *unintentionally* legislated out of existence."
—*Report of the United States Monetary Commission*, 1876.

General Grant, who signed the law, did not know that silver was demonetized. As late as the 14th January, 1875, he recommends the establishment of new mints, because the existing facilities would not suffice " to coin the *silver* necessary to transact the business of the country."

special law for demonetizing silver as in Germany, but by making use of the codification of the Mint laws in 1873 to insert an alteration forbidding the further coinage of the silver dollar.[1] When the people understood what had been done they demanded the reinstatement of silver. Numerous bills were brought in for the free coinage of that metal. As a result of a double amendment, an Act was finally passed on 28th February, 1878, providing for the limited coinage of the white metal. This act, known as the "Bland Bill," had to be carried over the veto of the President.

Unscientific, crude, and provisional as the Act is, it is still a grand achievement. It is the American declaration of independence of thought against the tyranny of European monetary theories and the monstrous and unjust doctrine of the English school of gold monometallism. It marks the beginning of a powerful reaction in America, of a struggle between the people and the confederated monopolists, the masses and the "vested wrongs" of those two powers which are the creation and the legacy of the great civil war, that of the National banks and that of the bondholders. This struggle is still going on and forms to-day perhaps the most prominent feature of American politics.

Ever since the Bland Bill was passed, the united gold-

---

[1] This did not affect the legal tender functions of the silver dollars already coined.

press of England[1] and America have worked hard to obtain its repeal ; but despite the large funds at the disposal of this agitation, the attempt has so far failed. Every means has been tried to obtain the desired object. The opponents of silver have posed as the champions of financial honesty, and have proclaimed that dollar which up to 1873 was the country's standard coin to be a "dishonest dollar." They have declared that to pay debts with this dollar is an "act of repudiation," "a flagrant breach of public faith."[2] They boycotted thas dollar so that it had to remain in the Treasury and then, under the plaudits of the gold press of Europe, called it "useless money." They have constituted themselves the advocates of the working man professing no other object than to insure the payment of his wages in dollars worth not less than 100 cents. They have secured the assistance of consecutive presidents and secretaries of the Treasury. But all in vain. The people distrusted this new fangled zeal of bankers and officials for their welfare. They knew that the executive was hostile to silver. Under capable leaders who fight the silver battle in congress bravely and well, they gather together and are now determined to demonstrate that in the end they will be stronger than Treasury officials,

[1] Nearly the whole English press is on the side of the American gold party. This adds considerably to the popularity of the silver men, who now are not only the champions of the rights of the people but of a *National American* policy.

[2] *Economist*, 24th July, 1886.

bankers, bank conventions and clearing houses. They are resolved to no longer assist other countries by the cheap export of one of their own productions—silver—to undersell the remainder of America's productions in the markets of the world, for though India might continue to export as much wheat, cotton, &c., after silver is reinstated, as she does now, she could do so only at higher gold prices.

The real strength of the silver party may be gleaned from the estimate of their opponents, from the fact that even those who wish to destroy the Bland Act find it politic to sail under the bi-metallic flag, and to propose its repeal, not in the interests of mono-metallism, but in that of bi-metallism.[1] The cessation of the future coinage of silver is recommended because bi-metallism can only triumph by adopting heroic measures; only when the panic and the cataclysm certain to follow the

[1] "International Union now seems hopeless while we continue to mitigate the diffculties of other nations by taking off the market half the product of our mines, which is nearly half the product of the world. Is it not worth while to try the results of an altered situation after so many years of failures ? Is it not worth while to see what can be done when the United States shall have put an end by stopping the coinage, to the charge that they are moved by selfish interests and trying to market their silver ? "—*D. Manning's Report*, 7th December, 1885. Again : " The only road to bi-metallism is by way of suspension and unconditional suspension. There is only one way, and one only, by which silver can be restored to its old ratio and value, namely, an international concert upon a common ratio with open mints to both metals at that ratio."—*D. Manning's Reply to questions addressed in Bland resolutions*, Washington, 2nd March, 1876.

suspension of the Bland Act, has taught England a severe lesson and has forced her, for the sake of India, to abandon her present anti-silver attitude.[1] Whether these recommendations are sincere or not we do not profess to know ; for us suffices the significant fact that such tactics are being adopted.

But in spite of all, the repeal of the Bland Act has not been carried, and as the discussion on this question extends, the people begin to understand more and more the whole bearing of this controversy and the result is an ever growing influence of the silver party. Relying only on these general considerations and without pretending to any special information we ventured to predict[2] the defeat of the agitation against the Bland Act at a time when papers like the "Times,"[3] the "Economist,"[4] and the "Statist,"[5] were informed that

, [1] "There is no need for our taking the position of a suppliant for favors. We can force action by simply suspending coinage."—*New York Chronicle*, 14th August, 1886.

[2] "The Future of Silver."—*Journal Institute of Bankers*, April, 1885.

[3] "That the further coinage of silver will cease must be looked upon as more than probable. That the Treasury will go on coining silver money for which it can find no use is perhaps more than the most hopeful of silver men can expect."—*Times*, 18th March, 1886.

[4] "The Americans are much too practical a people to endure long the operation of so pernicious a measure."—*Economist*, 7th March, 1885. Again : "For our own part we are inclined to believe that the silver coinage will be arrested."—*Economist*, 12th December, 1885.

[5] "We have good reason to believe that the course which we have steadily indicated of late as likely to be followed by the United States Congress in dealing with Bland Act will in fact be followed. We are assured by those most competent to form an opinion that the *banking interests* in the United States coinciding with the views and

this act was doomed.[1] The silver question is a peoples' question, though it may never become a popular one; it is a question between debtors and creditors, a question of the masses versus certain classes. It is the "war of the millions"—millions of people against millions of money. This point once thoroughly understood, there is little fear indeed, that in Modern democracies[2] the verdict will be given in favor of the limited number of the possessors of the mobilized wealth and against the interests of the toiling millions.[3]

But the Bland Act is essentially a provisional measure. When it was passed, it was no doubt hoped in more than one quarter, that Europe would follow the

plans of the Government and of influential members of the Democratic Party are now quite certain to prevail. In other words, it may be considered almost as good as settled that the Bland Act will be repealed."—*Statist*, 10th October, 1885. "We are inclined to think that it will be practicable" (*i.e.*, suspension of the silver coinage).—*Statist*, 12th December, 1885.

[1] The "World," however, almost alone correctly estimated the position of parties in the States, and predicted that the Bland Bill will *not* fall.

[2] The enlightened advocates of mono-metallism fully perceive this danger, and are afraid. "On a question of determining the ratio, think of going to the constituencies!"—*Speech of Mr. Harvey, Journal of Institute of Bankers*, June, 1886.

[3] In Germany, at the time the standard was changed, the people did not understand the point at issue. The old liabilities were converted at the rate of 1:15½, which Mr. Bamberger, the Parliamentary leader of the gold mono-metallists, declared fair, (speech in *Reichstag*, 11th November, 1871,) "because it is the average relation of the century to which gold and silver have always returned after disturbances." After the debts were so converted, Mr. Bamberger wrote his *Reichsgold*, and said that the fall in silver was an elemental and necessary fact of historic evolution.

example of the United States. This hope was disappointed. The new gold fashion was still too fresh to be changed quickly, and no doubt the fact that, in spite of this act, silver continued to fall, had also a deterring effect. There will be no difficulty in carrying out the Bland Act as it stands, and continuing the limited coinage of silver, for some years to come.[1] But the time must arrive when the present provisional enactments with regard to silver will have to be replaced by something more permanent and systematic. The question which is already casting its shadow before will then be, whether to abandon the present policy of giving silver a lift, or whether America in the full consciousness of her immense economic and financial strength will open her mints alone and unaided to the free coinage of silver and demonstrate to the whole world the fallacy of the mono-metallic doctrine by the success which is certain to attend such an experiment.

The counsellors who, in and out of Congress, advise the United States to follow this latter policy are growing in number and influence every day. They proclaim that the free coinage of silver is the logical outcome of the present position. They urge America "to show

---

[1] The provision attached last session (1886) to the Civil Appropriation Bill authorizing and requiring the issue of one, two, and five dollar silver certificates is a means of making the silver dollars, now idle in the Treasury, available, facilitating thus the working of the Bland Act. The silver dollars are a legal tender at their "nominal value for all debts and dues public and private," the silver dollar certificates are only "receivable for customs, taxes, and all public dues." But that suffices.

a manly example as one of the greatest and most powerful nations on the face of the earth, and to teach the erring commercial and industrial sister nations the right path to reach a sound metallic currency." They maintain— and there can be no doubt with perfect justification— that with their large productions of the precious metals, the United States are to-day strong enough by themselves to control the ratio of gold and· silver, and to dictate it to the world as did France previous to 1872, Spain after 1546, and Portugal after 1688. The boldness of such a step, which might deter other nations, seems to have a positive charm for the Americans.[1] " Our fathers " says a Congressional report[2] " when they adopted a constitutional standard of value based on gold and silver, when they gave free and unlimited coinage to both metals, never entertained the thought of asking the concurrence of other nations." And what, it is asserted, the small group of states that declared their independence 100 years ago were not obliged to do, the powerful continent of to-day with its teeming millions need not do at the present time. America possesses statesmen of bold action and great foresight who have

[1] "I do continually hear men in this country declaiming in one breath about the tottering thrones of Europe and the grandeur of liberty regulated by law here, and in the next insisting that our monetary system must conform to that of the great European powers. This will not do."—Speech in the United States Senate of Hon. T. M. Bowen, 8th March, 1886.

[2] *Minority Report of Committee on Coinage, Weights and Measures*, Washington, February, 1886.

thoroughly mastered all the bearings of this silver question and are quite prepared to countenance the free
coinage of silver in the United States without reference
to the legislation of Europe. By thus raising the price
of silver, by thus "intercepting the cheap supply of the
munitions of commercial war," the United States of
America would put an end to Indian competition at the
present low level of prices, and the American continent,
prosperous again, would attract anew in large numbers
fresh settlers from Europe.

Already in 1879 Mr. Bland said in Congress: "Mr.
Chairman, it is not to our interest for England or Germany to unite with us on this silver question. I maintain that so far as Germany and other countries are
demonetizing silver and banishing that metal from their
shores thus far are they driving their people also away.
I maintain further than in so far this government re-
monetizes silver and thereby revives business here we
draw to our shores the people of Germany and Great
Britain."

The free coinage of silver in the United States would
undoubtedly benefit the whole world, but the American
statesmen will unquestionably know how to arrange mat-
ters in such a way, as to secure to their own country the
lion's share of the advantages. It would be well for
English statesmen to bear this in mind. The thought
must seriously damp the joy which these devotees of
inactivity—which in this question has ever been the reverse

of masterly—might otherwise experience at the prospect of this question being settled by somebody else without any expense of brain and nerve power of their own. A bi-metallic America with a large stock of silver on hand would have advantages for trading with the East not enjoyed by England so long as she maintains the single gold standard, for England would have to buy silver at a premium. This advantage expressed in percentage may not be large, but it would tell in an age used to look after small differences. America might use this opportunity in order to obtain a share and probably an increasing share in the trade with the far East. Owning as she does a splendid continent, bathed by two mighty oceans, whose climate has every varying change, whose rivers flow through fertile valleys, peopled by an enterprising and energetic race, free from most of the political fears which overhang Europe, America only requires a controlling position in the Eastern trade to become the paramount power in the world, and to make New York the Empire city not of a nation but of the universe. The question which in this country becomes more urgent every day is: Will England allow her to acquire those advantages through the supineness of those who are called upon to watch over her destiny ?

We are, however, not here concerned with the question of who will eventually benefit most by the reinstatement of silver. Our enquiry extends simply into the chances of bi-metallism. Believing, as we do, that the final

victory of the gold party would be followed by un-
speakable misery, that it would upset commerce, that it
would destroy the social fabric built up with so much
care, and so far the only intelligible base of all further
economic development, that it would therefore arrest
the evolution of the human race, we are glad to find
that our survey of the situation leads us to the conclusion that the victory of bi-metallism in the United
States is but a question of a short time.

Whether this expectation will be realized or not,
events must show. Nor would the success or non-
success of the forecast here attempted in any way add
to, or detract from, any value which our remarks in the
principal and less ambitious portion of this treatise may
possess, the aim of which has been to establish, beyond
doubt and cavil, the connexion between the Silver
Question and our Social Future.

In an evil hour for humanity the idea of extending
the single gold standard to the whole world was con-
ceived. Since the day when Germany took the first step
towards the realization of this idea down to this time,
humanity has had to fight a continuous battle against
the evils resulting from this attempt. We have so far
escaped the great collapse that more than once threatened to crown years of losses and retrogression. But
he would be a bold man indeed who dared to predict
that this collapse is definitely averted. The elements of
financial danger are all around us. Nearly all states

except England temporize with that danger by count-
ing some of their silver as gold, and in England the
gold circulation and the gold reserve of the Bank have
alike declined.

In the course of this struggle for the single gold
standard, the *rôles* of the mono-metallists and the bi-
metallists have completely changed. The former are
now really fighting for the establishment of a dual
system of money which would divide the commercial
world into two hostile camps. The latter endeavour
to establish a system of the same monetary standard
for the whole universe. They are, therefore, to-day
the real representatives of monetary cosmopolitanism,
the true champions of a world-money.[1]

Bi-metallism does not claim to be a panacea for all
the evils that man is heir to. It is no magic wand with
which to conjure up bountiful harvests or with which to
ensure absolute certainty of business success. It is no
guarantee against over-speculation or commercial crises.
But it will give back stability of value to the moneys of

[1] " As the matter stands at present it seems to me that those who
are called bi-metallists are really mono-metallists. They try to·
marry the yellow and the white metal, to combine the two, and thus
to create a basis broad enough to carry on the ever increasing
commerce of the world, and to found upon it a stable system of
prices and a firm superstructure of credit. Those on the other hand
who are called mono-metallists are really bi-metallists. They want
to divorce silver from gold and cut the world into two parts with
no common measure of value between them."—Speech, *Journal
Institute of Bankers*, December, 1885.

the world, to the sovereign of the English as much as to
the rupee of the Hindoo, and it will save the innumer-
able social relations of life which are based on monetary
considerations from great and ever increasing disturbance.

There is no justification for the assertion that the introduction of bi-metallism would violently disturb existing trade relations. Certain precautions which will at
once suggest themselves to men of business, and into
which we need not enter here, would adequately safe-
guard all legitimate interests.

But even a temporary interference with trade, con-
fined as it would be to a single instance and within assignable limits, must be deemed a small price indeed to
pay for the cessation of the present constant fluctuations
between gold and silver and for the creation of a stable
international money that will suffice to serve the needs
of humanity for generations to come.

We are living in an age of no ordinary difficulties.
New and pressing social questions are coming to the
front and peremptorily demand a hearing. To answer
them satisfactorily we require the loyal co-operation of
all conservative elements of society. Such times allow
no longer of hesitancy, procrastination and timidity;
they demand courage and decision; they call for positive
and constructive statesmenship. More than all, they
impose upon our rulers the paramount duty of speedily
putting an end to the depreciation of silver, which

cancer-like is eating away the vital parts of our social organism; which by a silent revolution undermines the economic power and the political influence of those classes that have ever been the loyal supporters of the government and the crown; while, at the same time, as the ultimate cause of bad trade and scant employment, it is the most active agent of popular discontent, a constantly threatening danger to the whole structure of society, and the mainspring of that social insurrection the distant thunder of which is already audible in all the great centres of civilization.

www.ingramcontent.com/pod-product-compliance
Lightning Source LLC
Chambersburg PA
CBHW032248080426
42735CB00008B/1050